ART EXTENSIONS
CHRISTIAN ART MASTERPIECES
DRAWING AND COLORING BOOK

For Adults and Children including Art Appreciation and
Historical Background from Bible Stories and the Lives of the Saints

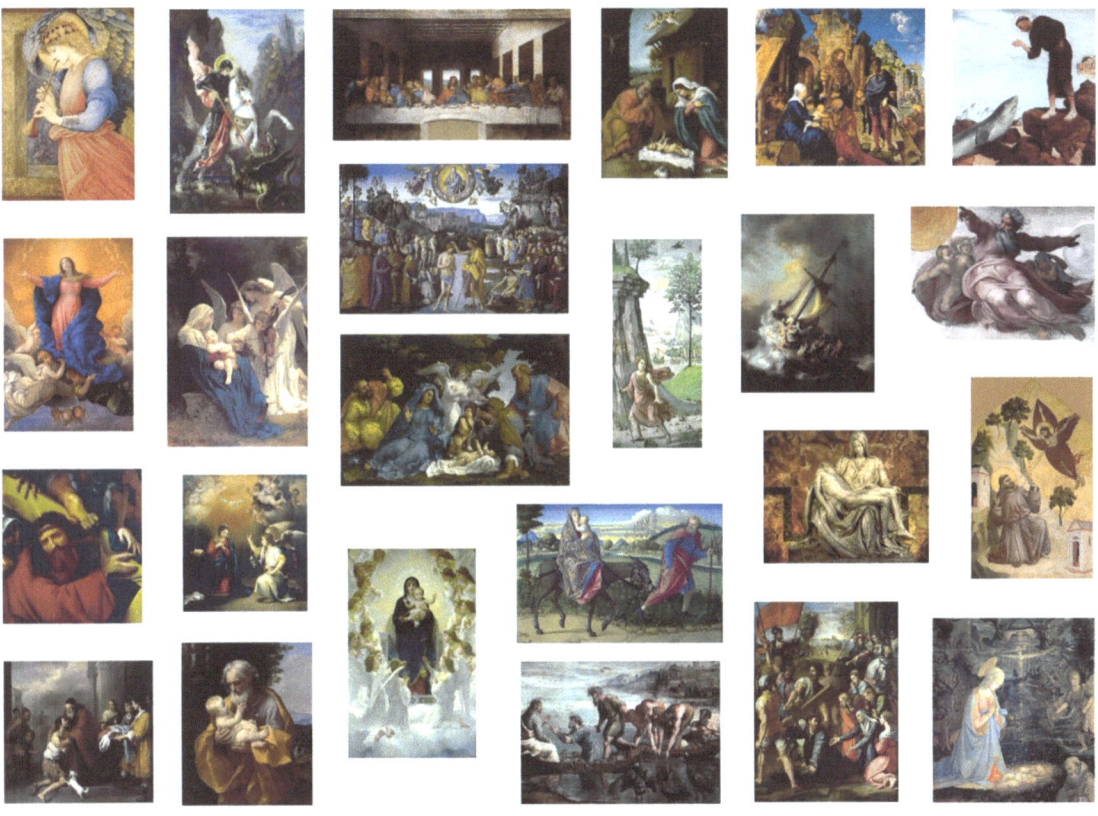

Kathryn Marcellino

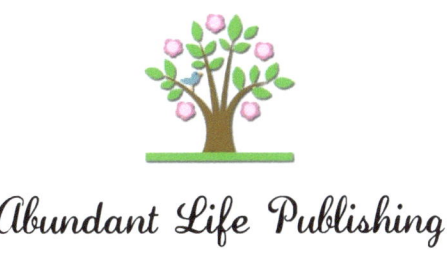

Abundant Life Publishing

Copyright ©2016 Kathryn Marcellino

Cover design, illustrations, and graphic design are by Kathryn Marcellino.
The art masterpieces in this book are in the public domain.
Scripture quotations used in this book are from the World English Bible unless otherwise noted.

A special thank you to Joan M. Lehman for her suggestions, research, and help in editing this book.

Disclaimer: Background research has revealed some differences between sources. We chose to use sources that seemed the most authoritative, but we cannot guarantee that all information is accurate including the current location of the paintings.

No part of this book except the public domain portions may be reproduced, stored in a retrieval system, or transmitted in any form, or by any means, electronic, mechanical, photocopying, or otherwise, without the prior written permission of the author, except by a reviewer who may quote brief passages in a review. Permission is also given to those who purchase this book to copy pages for the use of themselves and immediate family members.

ISBN 978-1-944158-02-6 (Paperback)

Abundant Life Publishing
PO Box 3753
Modesto, CA 95352
Email: km@AbundantLifePublishing.com

www.AbundantLifePublishing.com

Printed in the USA

Other books by Kathryn Marcellino include:

Jesse Tree Ornaments: Advent Coloring Activities and Craft Projects for Kids with Bible Stories

Twenty Mysteries of the Rosary Coloring Book

Rosary Meditations: The Gospel in Miniature

Christian Cathedrals Stained Glass Coloring Book for Adults and Children

How to Pray the Rosary as a Pathway to Contemplation

Table of Contents

About this Book 4

Examples of Art Extensions 5

Art Extensions to Draw and Color (with Background Information):

An Angel Playing a Flageolet by Edward Burne-Jones 6

The Creation of the Sun, Moon, and Planets by Michelangelo 8

Saint John the Baptist in the Desert by Domenico Ghirlandaio 10

Annunciation to the Virgin by Bartolomé Esteban Murillo 12

Nativity of Christ by Lorenzo Lotto 14

Adoration of the Child with Saints by Filippo Lippi 16

Adoration of the Magi by Albrecht Durer 18

Song of the Angels by William-Adolphe Bouguereau 20

The Flight into Egypt by Vittore Carpaccio 22

Holy Family with Angels by Lorenzo Lotto 24

Saint Joseph with the Infant Jesus by Guido Reni 26

Baptism of Christ by Pietro Perugino 28

The Return of the Prodigal Son by Bartolome Esteban Murillo 30

Christ in the Storm on the Sea of Galilee by Rembrandt 32

Miraculous Draught of Fishes by Raphael 34

The Last Supper by Leonardo da Vinci 36

Christ Carrying the Cross by Lorenzo Lotto 38

Christ Falls on the Route to Calvary by Raphael 40

Pietà by Michelangelo 42

Assumption of the Virgin Mary by Guido Reni 44

Saint Francis of Assisi Receiving the Stigmata by Giotto 46

Saint George and the Dragon by Gustave Moreau 48

Saint Anthony Preaching to the Fish by Arnold Böcklin 50

The Queen of the Angels or The Virgin with Angels by William-Adolphe Bouguereau 52

About this Book

This book is the original art extension drawing and coloring book that was inspired by a type of art project that the author enjoyed back in the 1960s when art classes were a part of the regular curriculum in grammar school. This book focuses on Christian paintings and includes historical background information including the religious significance of the subject matter with some Bible quotations and stories from the lives of the saints.

The art activities in this book are a combination of drawing, coloring, art appreciation, and art history. Each art extension in this book begins with a color reproduction of a great art masterpiece, which is centered on a larger page. Then by drawing freehand and coloring one extends the painting around the edges to match or accent the artwork. Using one's imagination and creativity, one can extend the original art in a variety ways. For example, if there is a river in the original painting, it could continue out to border, bend and flow behind hill, or whatever one imagines. As an alternative one could color in highlights or designs in the background. There are really no rules, but the original idea of an art extension was to match the style and colors of the art masterpiece so that one could hardly tell where the original artwork ends and the extension begins.

The author hopes each person using this book will draw and color what inspires them. One can use any choice of colors or designs. Many types of coloring media may be used from colored pencils, crayons, felt tip markers, to pastels. It is good to pick a media that can be blended or has many different color choices in order to match the original such as a set of colored pencils or a large box of crayons with many shades and colors.

The following pages include miniatures of art masterpieces from some of the world's most famous artists such as Leonardo Da Vinci, Michelangelo, Rembrandt, and many more. Below and on the next page are some examples of art extensions using a few masterpieces in this book.

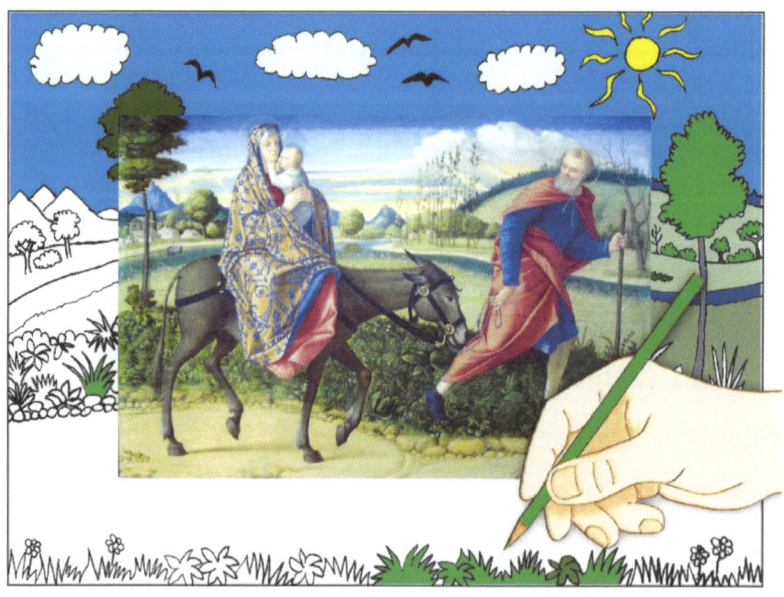

Examples of Art Extensions

The original art masterpiece is on the left, with an example of a corresponding art extension on the right.

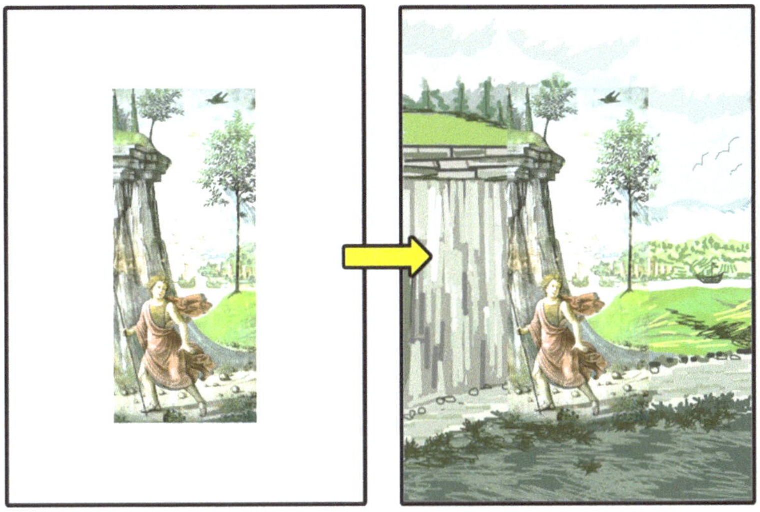

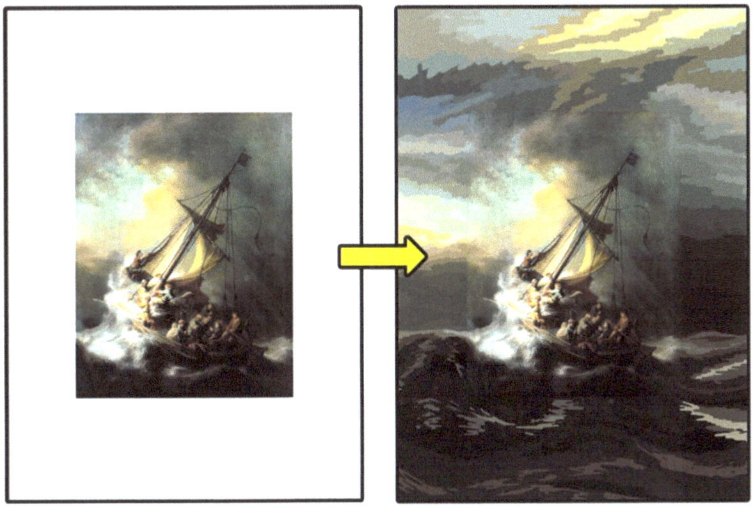

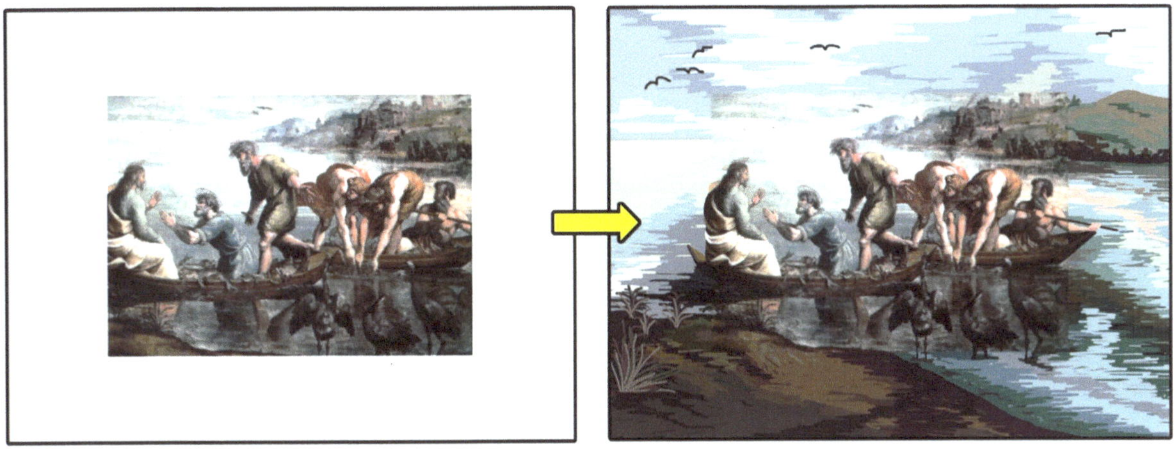

Draw and color your own art extensions on the following pages....

An Angel Playing a Flageolet

Artist: Edward Burne-Jones
Date: 1878
Media: tempera and gold paint on paper
Style or Movement: Romanticism
Current location: Sudley House, Liverpool, England
⇨

Sir Edward Coley Burne-Jones (1833-1898) was a British artist and designer who worked on a wide range of decorative arts including stained glass. Burne-Jones had a vivid imagination and wrote to a friend: "I mean by a picture a beautiful, romantic dream of something that never was, never will be—in a light better than any light that ever shone—in a land no one can define or remember, only desire—and the forms divinely beautiful . . . " (Hugh Chrisholm, *The Encyclopaedia Britannica: A Dictionary of Arts, Sciences, Literature and General Information,* New York: University Press, 1910).

Burne-Jones was an artist associated with Romanticism, which is an expansive and hard-to-define movement that peaked around 1800 to 1850. The Romantic era was an artistic, musical, literary, and intellectual period that was characterized by its emphasis on the intense personal expression of emotion and imagination.

In this painting the light shining on the face, hands, and heart of the angel emphasizes the intense focus, thoughtfulness, and peace with which the heavenly song is played. The complementary colors of orange and blue in the clothing, and the curved lines of the fabric folds and wing feathers contrast with the straight lines of the background add complexity to the painting.

Religious significance of the subject matter: Angels are messengers sent by God.

Angels are spirit beings but are often depicted in art as having human form with the addition of elements such as birdlike wings, halos, and light. Angels were created before human beings and are greater than human beings including being more intelligent. "What is man that you think of him? Or the son of man that you care for him? You made him a little lower than the angels. You crowned him with glory and honor" (Hebrews 2:6-7).

The word "angel" is mentioned 273 times in the Bible (World English Bible version), and angels play an important role in Scripture. Angels are regarded as messengers of God and have various activities and missions. The Bible mentions some of the names of individual angels such as Gabriel, Michael, and Raphael. There are also various categories of angels including the Seraphim, Cherubim, and Archangels. The Bible mentions many interactions between angels and humans including these below:

> An angel of the Lord appeared to him, standing on the right side of the altar of incense. Zacharias was troubled when he saw him, and fear fell upon him. But the angel said to him, "Don't be afraid, Zacharias, because your request has been heard, and your wife, Elizabeth, will bear you a son, and you shall call his name John." (Luke 1:11-13, World English Bible)

> Now in the sixth month, the angel Gabriel was sent from God to a city of Galilee, named Nazareth, to a virgin pledged to be married to a man whose name was Joseph, of David's house. The virgin's name was Mary. (Luke 1:26-27)

> There were shepherds in the same country staying in the field, and keeping watch by night over their flock. Behold, an angel of the Lord stood by them, and the glory of the Lord shone around them, and they were terrified. The angel said to them, "Don't be afraid, for behold, I bring you good news of great joy which will be to all the people. For there is born to you today, in David's city, a Savior, who is Christ the Lord. (Luke 2:8-11)

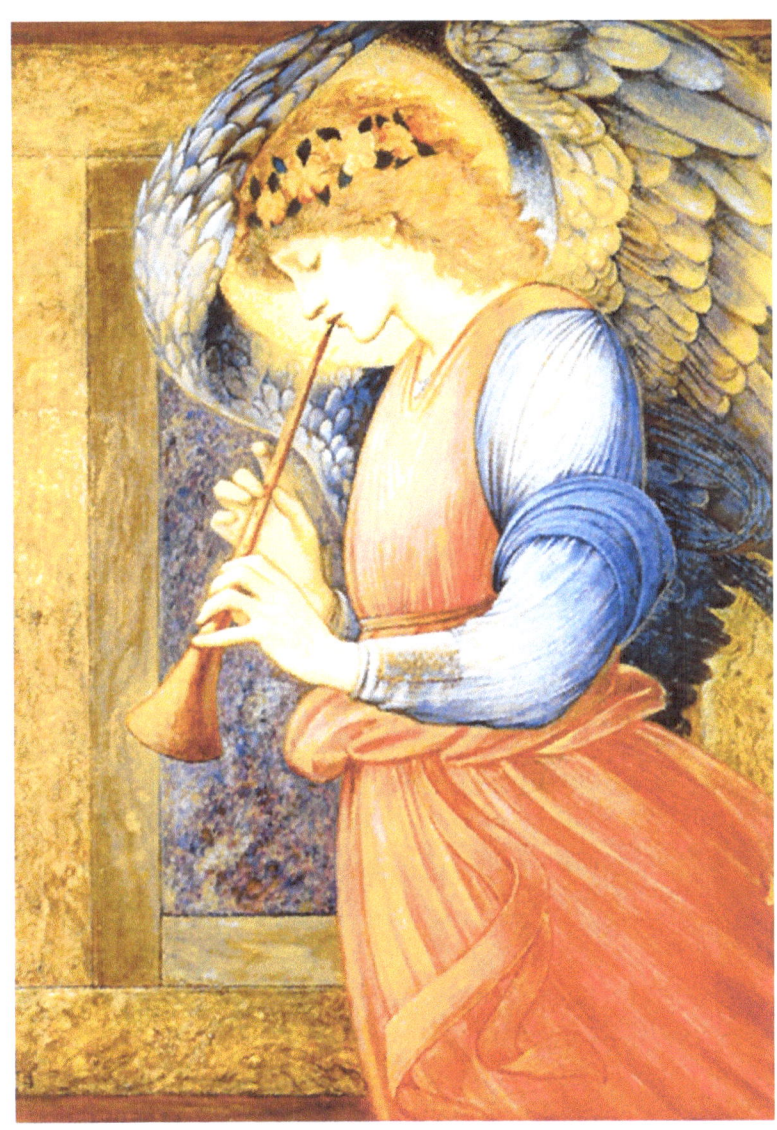

The Creation of the Sun, Moon, and Planets

Artist: Michelangelo
Date: circa 1511
Media: Fresco
Style or Movement: High Renaissance
Current location: Sistine Chapel, Vatican City
⇨

Michelangelo di Lodovico Buonarroti Simoni (1475-1564), popularly known simply as Michelangelo, was an Italian sculptor, painter, architect, poet, and engineer. He is described as one of the greatest artists of all time. His works in painting, sculpture, and architecture rank among the most famous in existence.

This image is a part of one of the nine frescos on the Book of Genesis located on the ceiling of the Sistine Chapel (located in the Vatican's Apostolic Palace, the official residence of the Pope). Fresco is a technique of mural painting where water is used to merge the pigment into wet lime plaster incorporating the image into the wall itself as the plaster sets.

In this fresco God's face expresses the force and divine energy of creation as he hurls the sun and moon into the sky in opposite directions. The drapery of the clothing dramatizes the motion of his effort and the strength of his form while the angels watch in awe of God's power.

Religious significance of the subject matter: God is Creator of the universe and all things in it.

The Book of Genesis in the Bible recounts the story of God creating the universe and all things in it. This particular artwork depicts Genesis when God created the sun, moon, and stars on the fourth day as follows:

> God said, "Let there be lights in the expanse of sky to divide the day from the night; and let them be for signs to mark seasons, days, and years; and let them be for lights in the expanse of sky to give light on the earth"; and it was so. God made the two great lights: the greater light to rule the day, and the lesser light to rule the night. He also made the stars. God set them in the expanse of sky to give light to the earth, and to rule over the day and over the night, and to divide the light from the darkness. God saw that it was good. (Genesis 1: 14-18)

> The God who made the world and all things in it, he, being Lord of heaven and earth, doesn't dwell in temples made with hands, neither is he served by men's hands, as though he needed anything, seeing he himself gives to all life and breath, and all things. (Acts 17:24-25)

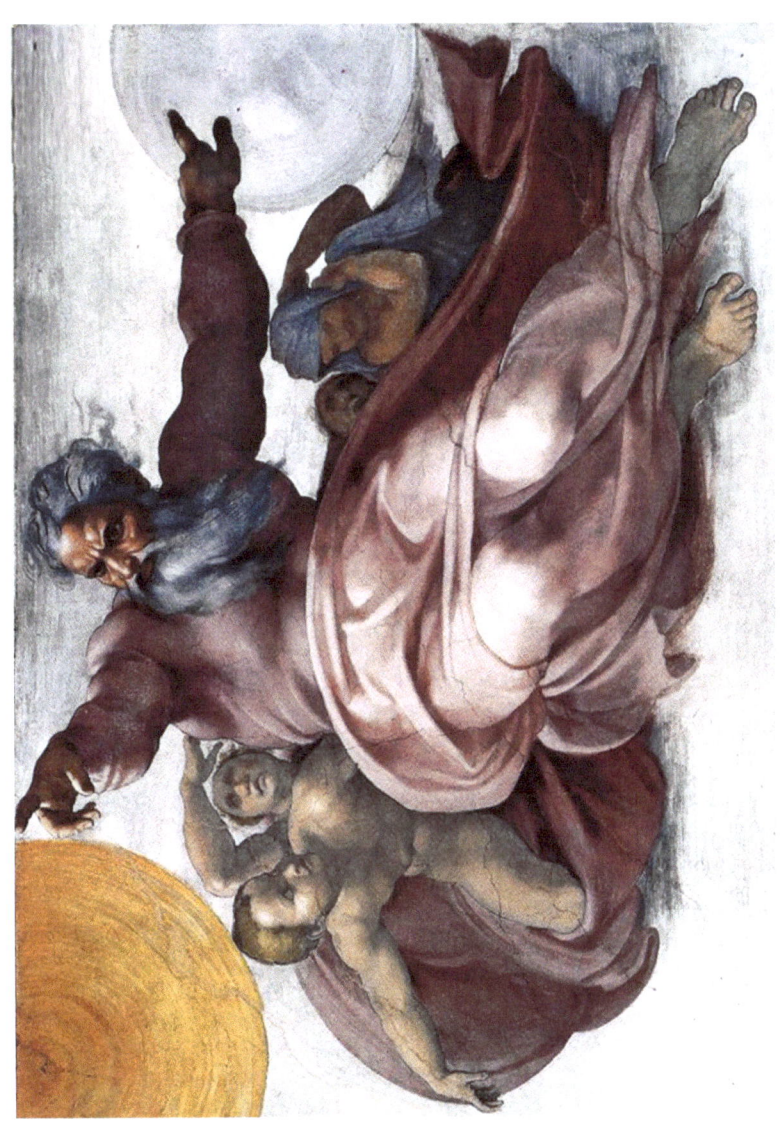

Saint John the Baptist in the Desert

Artist: Domenico Ghirlandaio
Date: circa 1486-1490
Media: Fresco
Style or Movement: Early Renaissance
Current location: Tornabuoni Chapel, Santa Maria Novella, Florence, Italy
➪

Domenico Ghirlandaio (1449-1494) was a very active and creative painter from Florence working mainly in fresco. Ghirlandaio was the leader of a large workshop, and Michelangelo was one of his many apprentices.

The Early Renaissance was an experimental period in the early 15th century when artists broke away from the restrictions of Byzantine Art. This era is characterized by great creative and intellectual activity.

In this narrow fresco we see a young John the Baptist turning to look back at his past as he hurries to turn a corner into the desert, perhaps with no return. The stark, angular rocks of the desert is suggestive of John's future in the desert living on locusts and wild honey, and is in sharp contrast with the lush, green world of the town, which is suggestive of a luxurious past.

Religious significance of the subject matter: John the Baptist preaches in the wilderness.

John the Baptist had a special role to play as one who was to prepare the way of the Lord.

> An angel of the Lord appeared to him, standing on the right side of the altar of incense. Zacharias was troubled when he saw him, and fear fell upon him. But the angel said to him, "Don't be afraid, Zacharias, because your request has been heard, and your wife, Elizabeth, will bear you a son, and you shall call his name John. You will have joy and gladness; and many will rejoice at his birth. For he will be great in the sight of the Lord, and he will drink no wine nor strong drink. He will be filled with the Holy Spirit, even from his mother's womb. He will turn many of the children of Israel to the Lord, their God. He will go before him in the spirit and power of Elijah, 'to turn the hearts of the fathers to the children,' and the disobedient to the wisdom of the just; to prepare a people prepared for the Lord."
> Zacharias said to the angel, "How can I be sure of this? For I am an old man, and my wife is well advanced in years."
> The angel answered him, "I am Gabriel, who stands in the presence of God. I was sent to speak to you, and to bring you this good news. Behold, you will be silent and not able to speak, until the day that these things will happen, because you didn't believe my words, which will be fulfilled in their proper time." (Luke 1:11-20)

> In those days, John the Baptizer came, preaching in the wilderness of Judea, saying, "Repent, for the Kingdom of Heaven is at hand!" For this is he who was spoken of by Isaiah the prophet, saying, "The voice of one crying in the wilderness, make ready the way of the Lord. Make his paths straight." Now John himself wore clothing made of camel's hair, with a leather belt around his waist. His food was locusts and wild honey. Then people from Jerusalem, all of Judea, and all the region around the Jordan went out to him. They were baptized by him in the Jordan, confessing their sins. (Matthew 3:1-6)

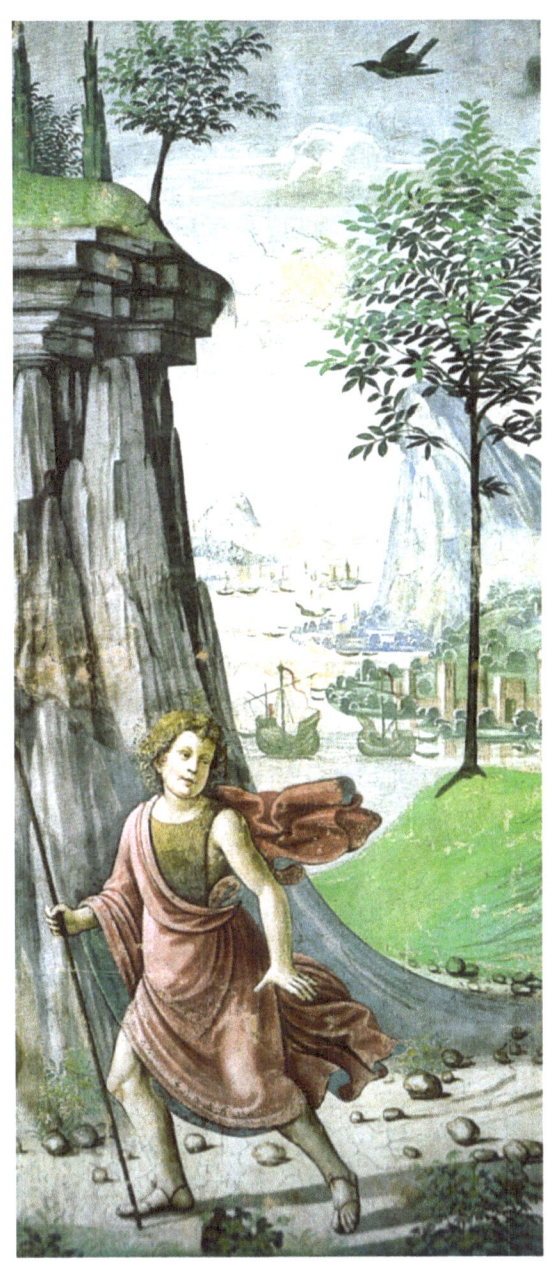

Annunciation to the Virgin

Artist: Bartolomé Esteban Murillo
Date: 1660-1680
Media: oil on canvas
Style or Movement: Baroque
Current location: Rijksmuseum, Amsterdam

Bartolomé Esteban Murillo (1618-1682) was a highly successful painter and is regarded as one of the leading Spanish Baroque artists. Murillo's style is soft, tender, and sentimental. He is known as the painter of sweetness and light.

The Baroque style used clear, exaggerated detail to depict motion, which produced drama and grandeur in the artwork. Baroque style art was commissioned by the Catholic Church to reassert itself in the wake of the Protestant Reformation.

This painting depicts a heavenly light that almost explodes on the divine moment when the Angel Gabriel reveals to Mary her most holy purpose. Gabriel appears almost as worldly as Mary except for his wings and flowing garments and seems to direct the descending dove towards the humble figure of Mary. The delight of frolicking, swirling angels seem to be in direct contrast to the serious nature of miracle.

Religious significance of the subject matter: The angel Gabriel appeared to Mary and told her that she had been chosen to be the mother of Jesus.

> Now in the sixth month, the angel Gabriel was sent from God to a city of Galilee, named Nazareth, to a virgin pledged to be married to a man whose name was Joseph, of the house of David. The virgin's name was Mary. Having come in, the angel said to her, "Rejoice, you highly favored one! The Lord is with you. Blessed are you among women!" But when she saw him, she was greatly troubled at the saying, and considered what kind of salutation this might be.
> The angel said to her, "Don't be afraid, Mary, for you have found favor with God. Behold, you will conceive in your womb, and bring forth a son, and will call his name 'Jesus.' He will be great, and will be called the Son of the Most High. The Lord God will give him the throne of his father, David, and he will reign over the house of Jacob forever. There will be no end to his Kingdom."
> Mary said to the angel, "How can this be, seeing I am a virgin?"
> The angel answered her, "The Holy Spirit will come on you, and the power of the Most High will overshadow you. Therefore also the holy one who is born from you will be called the Son of God. Behold, Elizabeth, your relative, also has conceived a son in her old age; and this is the sixth month with her who was called barren. ³⁷ For everything spoken by God is possible."
> Mary said, "Behold, the handmaid of the Lord; be it to me according to your word." The angel departed from her. (Luke 1:26-38)

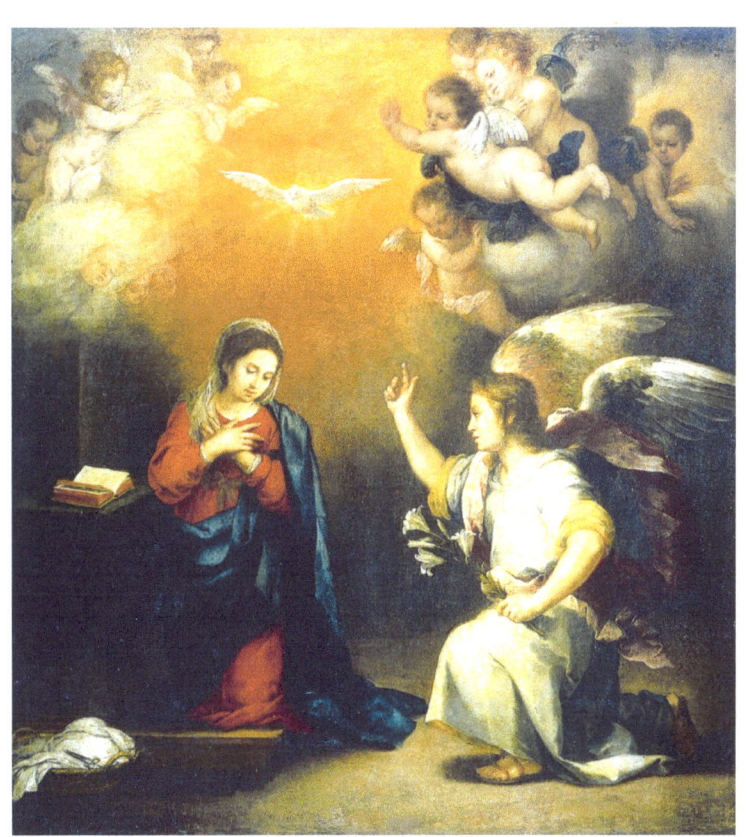

Nativity of Christ

Artist: Lorenzo Lotto
Date: 1523
Media: oil on panel
Style or Movement: High Renaissance
Current location: The National Gallery of Art, Washington, DC
➪

Lorenzo Lotto (about 1480-1556/7) was a leading Italian portrait and religious painter in the early 16th century. He was deeply religious and had an individual style compared to his contemporaries. His later paintings became extremely spiritual.

High Renaissance denotes the climax of the visual arts of the Italian Renaissance, traditionally taken to begin in the 1490s and ending in 1527 with the sacking of Rome.

This painting depicts a glowing crucifix on the wall depicting the manner of the infant's death overshadowing a tender loving moment of the Holy Family. As one looks closer, the eyes of Mary and Joseph gaze on the infant reaching up to his mother for love and protection. Angels hover above perhaps reading prophecies that will be fulfilled.

Religious significance of the subject matter: The birth of the Jesus Christ, the Son of God, is significant in that one of the three persons of the one true God became a man in order to save people from their sins and to give eternal life to those who choose to believe in Him.

> Now it happened in those days that a decree went out from Caesar Augustus that all the world should be enrolled. This was the first enrollment made when Quirinius was governor of Syria. All went to enroll themselves, everyone to his own city. Joseph also went up from Galilee, out of the city of Nazareth, into Judea, to the city of David, which is called Bethlehem, because he was of the house and family of David; to enroll himself with Mary, who was pledged to be married to him as wife, being pregnant. It happened, while they were there, that the day had come that she should give birth. She brought forth her firstborn son, and she wrapped him in bands of cloth, and laid him in a feeding trough, because there was no room for them in the inn. (Luke 2:1-7)

> The thief only comes to steal, kill, and destroy. I came that they may have life, and may have it abundantly. (John 10:10)

> In the beginning was the Word, and the Word was with God, and the Word was God. The same was in the beginning with God. All things were made through him. Without him was not anything made that has been made. In him was life, and the life was the light of men. The light shines in the darkness, and the darkness hasn't overcome it. There came a man, sent from God, whose name was John. The same came as a witness, that he might testify about the light, that all might believe through him. He was not the light, but was sent that he might testify about the light. The true light that enlightens everyone was coming into the world. He was in the world, and the world was made through him, and the world didn't recognize him. He came to his own, and those who were his own didn't receive him. But as many as received him, to them he gave the right to become God's children, to those who believe in his name: who were born not of blood, nor of the will of the flesh, nor of the will of man, but of God. The Word became flesh, and lived among us. We saw his glory, such glory as of the one and only Son of the Father, full of grace and truth. (John 1:1-14)

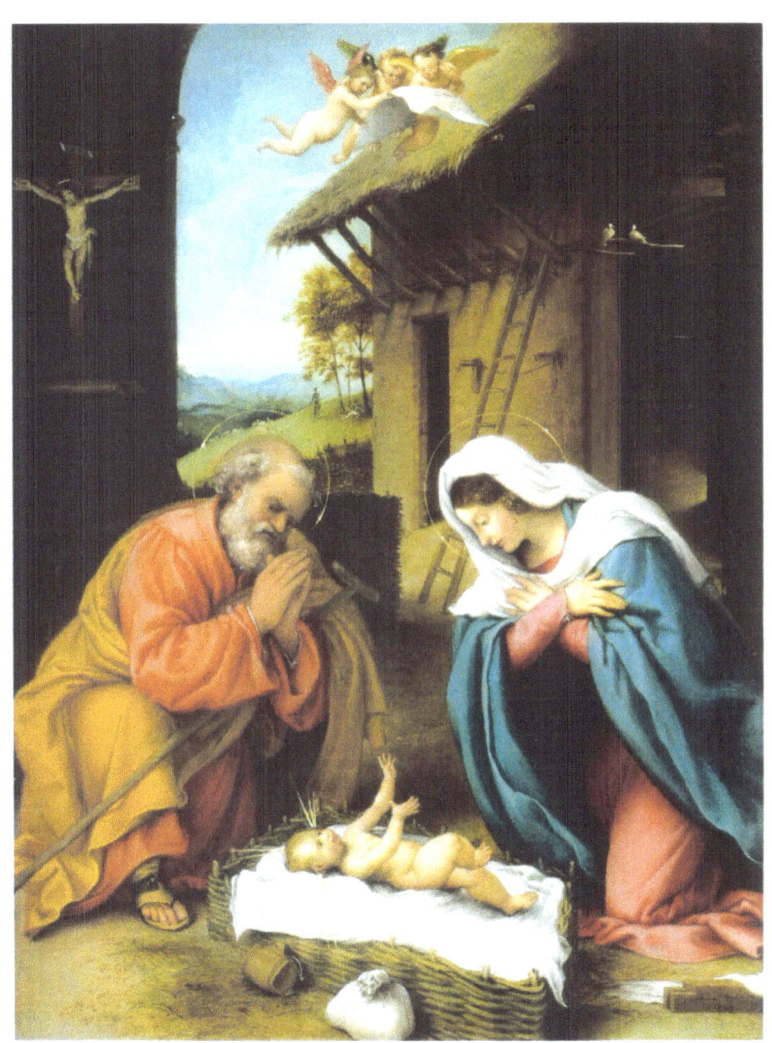

Adoration of the Child with Saints

Artist: Filippo Lippi
Date: circa 1463
Media: tempera on wood
Style or Movement: Early Renaissance
Current location: Uffizi Gallery, Florence, Italy
⇨

Filippo Lippi (1406-1469) was a Florentine painter in the second generation of the Renaissance artists. His work achieved a distinctive clarity of expression and presentation of reality. He led an adventurous life. He was orphaned, held as a slave, and became a priest who fell in love with a nun. He was arrested and tortured then was released from his vows and allowed to marry. The union produced a son, Filippino Lippi, who became another famous painter.

This painting was done using tempera on wood. Tempera is a fast-drying permanent painting medium that is a mixture of colored pigments and a water-soluble binder such as egg yolk.

This painting shows Mary in devotion to her child brilliantly glowing in a divine light, which is in sharp contrast to the background of a dark wooded landscape. God the Father's hands seem to direct the Holy Spirit to descend as a dove upon the baby Jesus. The saints looking lovingly at the Divine Infant may represent all believers who also adore Jesus as the Son of God.

Religious significance of the subject matter: Adoration of Baby Jesus

Before Jesus was conceived, Mary was told by the angel Gabriel that she would miraculously conceive and give birth to the Messiah, even though she was a virgin, and her son would be called Jesus and the Son of God.

When we look at Mary in the painting, we can almost hear Mary's words recorded in Scripture as quoted below.

> Mary said, "My soul magnifies the Lord.
> My spirit has rejoiced in God my Savior,
> for he has looked at the humble state of his servant.
> For behold, from now on, all generations will call me blessed.
> For he who is mighty has done great things for me. Holy is his name.
> His mercy is for generations of generations on those who fear him.
> He has shown strength with his arm.
> He has scattered the proud in the imagination of their hearts.
> He has put down princes from their thrones. And has exalted the lowly.
> He has filled the hungry with good things. He has sent the rich away empty.
> He has given help to Israel, his servant, that he might remember mercy,
> As he spoke to our fathers, to Abraham and his offspring forever." (Luke 1:46-55)

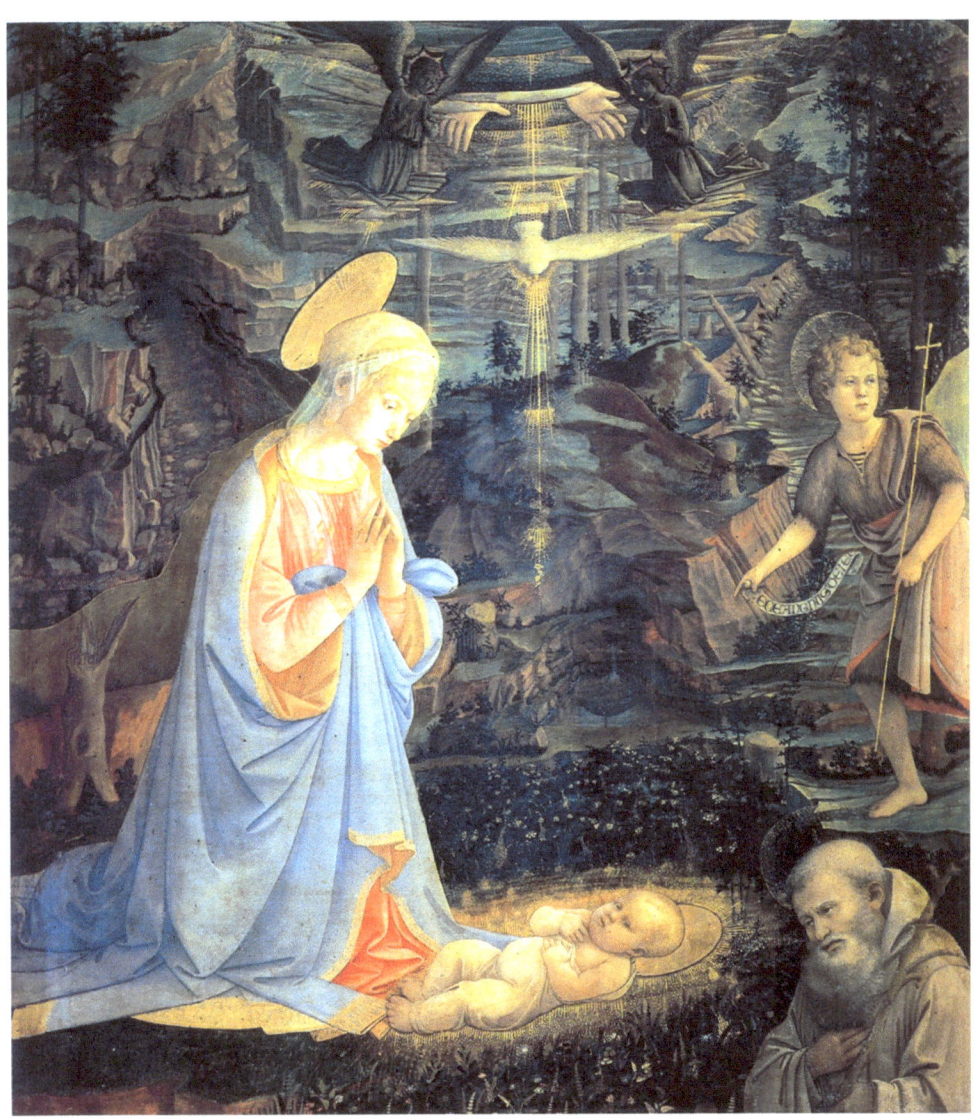

Adoration of the Magi

Artist: Albrecht Durer
Date: 1504
Media: oil on wood
Style or Movement: German Renaissance
Current Location: Uffizi Gallery, Florence, Italy
⇨

Albrecht Dürer (1471–1528) was a gifted and versatile German painter. He had much success in printmaking and engraving and was regarded as the greatest of the German Renaissance artists. His works included altarpieces, portraits, and copper engravings.

German Renaissance (part of the Northern Renaissance) developed from the Italian Renaissance in the 15th and 16th centuries. At the beginning of the 16th century, Germany was one of the most prosperous countries in Europe.

This painting is exquisite, meticulous in detail, and splendid in its color sense. The background perfectly frames the lavish kings bearing precious gifts to the Christ Child as he takes the hand of the eldest king. The Madonna is both beautiful and imaginative, and the livestock exceptionally lifelike. There is a notable omission of Joseph.

Religious significance of the subject matter: Adoration of the baby Jesus by the Wise Men

Jesus, the newborn King of the Jews, came not only for the Jews but for all people. The Wise Men, also called the Magi, represent the Gentiles (i.e., non-Jews) who would also come to believe in Jesus as the Messiah.

> Now when Jesus was born in Bethlehem of Judea in the days of King Herod, behold, wise men from the east came to Jerusalem, saying, "Where is he who is born King of the Jews? For we saw his star in the east, and have come to worship him."
> When King Herod heard it, he was troubled, and all Jerusalem with him. Gathering together all the chief priests and scribes of the people, he asked them where the Christ would be born. They said to him, "In Bethlehem of Judea, for this is written through the prophet, 'You Bethlehem, land of Judah, are in no way least among the princes of Judah: for out of you shall come forth a governor, who shall shepherd my people, Israel.'"
> Then Herod secretly called the wise men, and learned from them exactly what time the star appeared. He sent them to Bethlehem, and said, "Go and search diligently for the young child. When you have found him, bring me word, so that I also may come and worship him."
> They, having heard the king, went their way; and behold, the star, which they saw in the east, went before them, until it came and stood over where the young child was. When they saw the star, they rejoiced with exceedingly great joy. They came into the house and saw the young child with Mary, his mother, and they fell down and worshiped him. Opening their treasures, they offered to him gifts: gold, frankincense, and myrrh. Being warned in a dream that they shouldn't return to Herod, they went back to their own country another way. (Matthew 2:1-12)

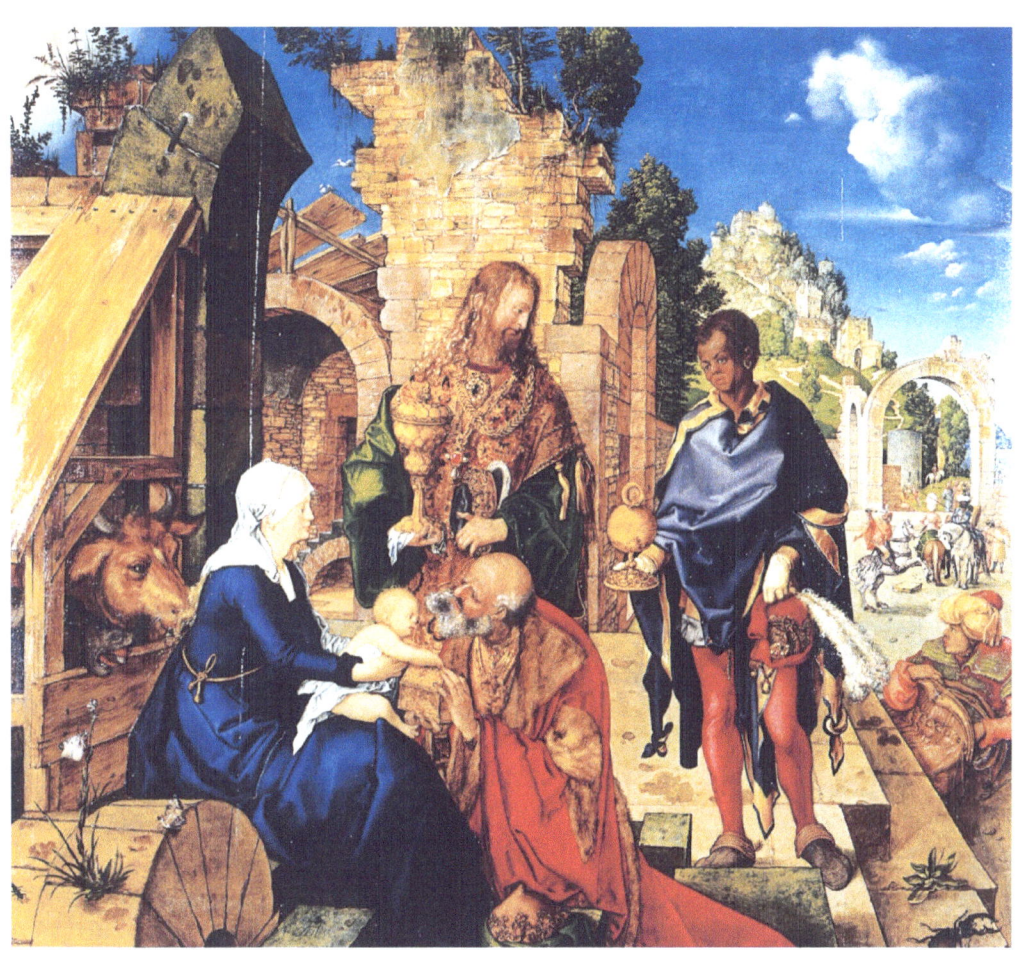

Song of the Angels

Artist: William-Adolphe Bouguereau
Date: 1881
Media: oil on canvas
Style or Movement: Neoclassicism
Current Location: Forest Lawn Museum, Glendale, California
⇨

William-Adolphe Bouguereau (1825-1905) was a French academic painter and a staunch Traditionalist with over 800 finished works. His emphasis was on the female form, and his paintings were noted for their realism. He received many commissions to decorate private houses, public buildings, and churches.

Neoclassicism drew its inspiration from the classical art and culture of ancient Greece and ancient Rome. The movement coincided with the Age of Enlightenment in the mid 18th century and continued until the early 19th century when it competed with Romanticism.

This painting was restored at the J. Paul Getty Museum beginning in 2005. It is a life-size depiction of a peaceful sleeping infant Jesus in the arms of his graceful loving Mother being serenaded by a trio of attentively serene angels in beautiful, flawless perfection.

Religious significance of the subject matter: Mary lovingly holds her son Jesus with angels gazing on attentively.

The artist representation brings to mind that we are not only physical bodies in a physical universe, but there is also a supernatural dimension to us and the universe.

During his earthly ministry, Jesus mentioned the angels of children in Matthew 18:10: "See that you don't despise one of these little ones, for I tell you that in heaven their angels always see the face of my Father who is in heaven." If this applies to each child, so much more can we conclude that the child Jesus would be constantly surrounded by angels as represented in the painting.

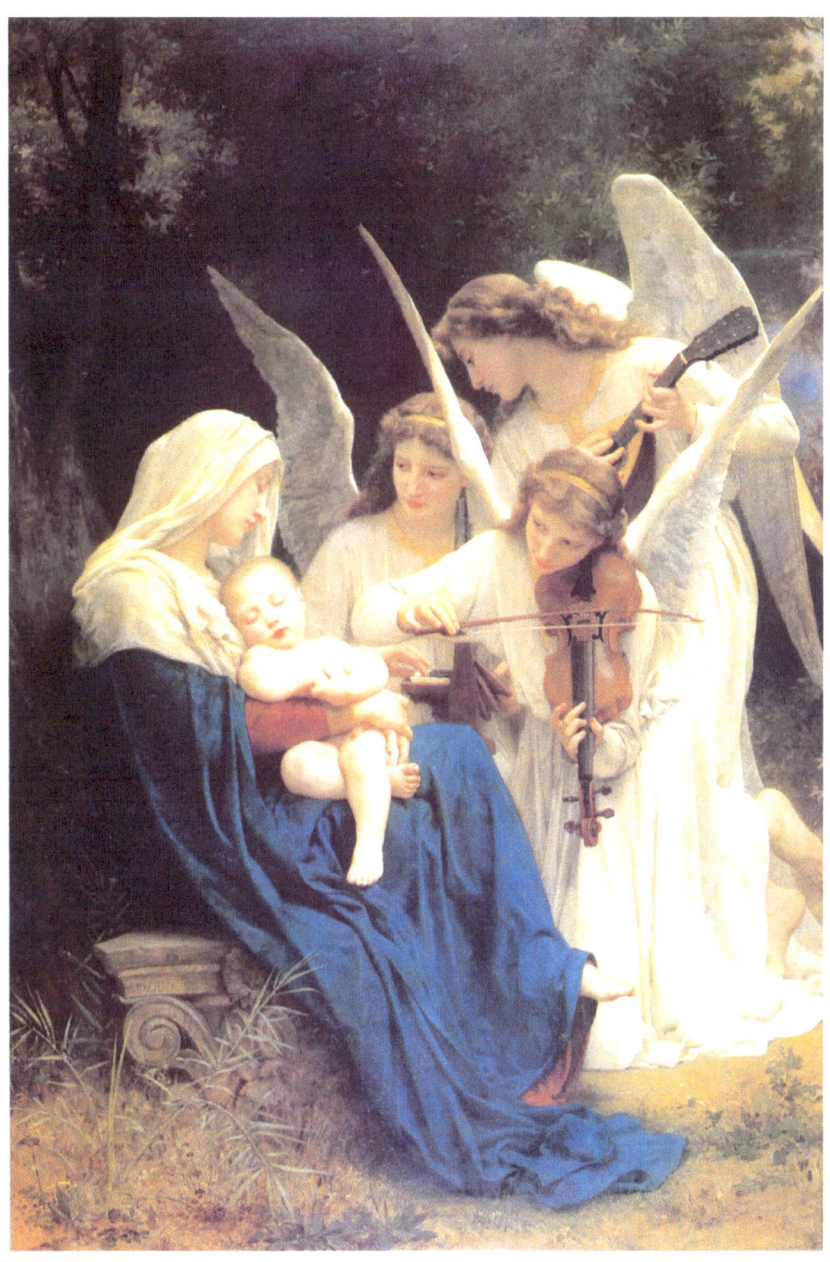

The Flight into Egypt

Artist: Vittore Carpaccio
Date: circa 1515
Media: oil on panel
Style or Movement: Italian Renaissance
Current Location: National Gallery of Art, Washington DC
⇨

Vittore Carpaccio (1460-1525/6) was the considered the greatest early Renaissance narrative painter of the Venetian school. His paintings were noted for their realistic detail, sunny coloring, and attention to costumes.

Italian Renaissance was a period of great cultural change and achievement that began in Italy during the 14th century and lasted until the 16th century. It was the earliest of the general European Renaissance marking the transition from Medieval to Early Modern Europe.

This vibrant, colorful painting shows an idealistic landscape that dominates the mood and character of the whole painting. The matching colors of Joseph and Mary's garments tie the protective couple together as a unit, but the exquisite detail of Mary's robe sets her apart as someone special.

Religious significance of the subject matter: The flight into Egypt of Jesus, Mary, and Joseph

After Jesus was born, King Herod, who the Romans had appointed king of the Jews, wanted to destroy him. The Three Kings (known also as the Wise Men or Magi) had told Herod of Christ's birth in Bethlehem as the prophets foretold. The Old Testament prophecies stated that the coming Messiah would be a king in the line of David. If Jesus indeed was the Messiah as the Wise Men thought then that would make Jesus the newborn king of the Jews. Herod perceived this as a threat to his own throne not realizing that Jesus's kingdom was not of this world (John 18:36). As a result Herod ordered all the baby boys in the area of Bethlehem to be killed hoping to kill Jesus too. Because of Herod's evil plan, an angel appeared to Joseph in a dream to warn him to take Jesus and Mary to Egypt until it was safe to return. This event is called "the flight into Egypt."

> Now when they had departed, behold, an angel of the Lord appeared to Joseph in a dream, saying, "Arise and take the young child and his mother, and flee into Egypt, and stay there until I tell you, for Herod will seek the young child to destroy him." He arose and took the young child and his mother by night, and departed into Egypt, and was there until the death of Herod; that it might be fulfilled which was spoken by the Lord through the prophet, saying, "Out of Egypt I called my son." (Matthew 2:13-15)

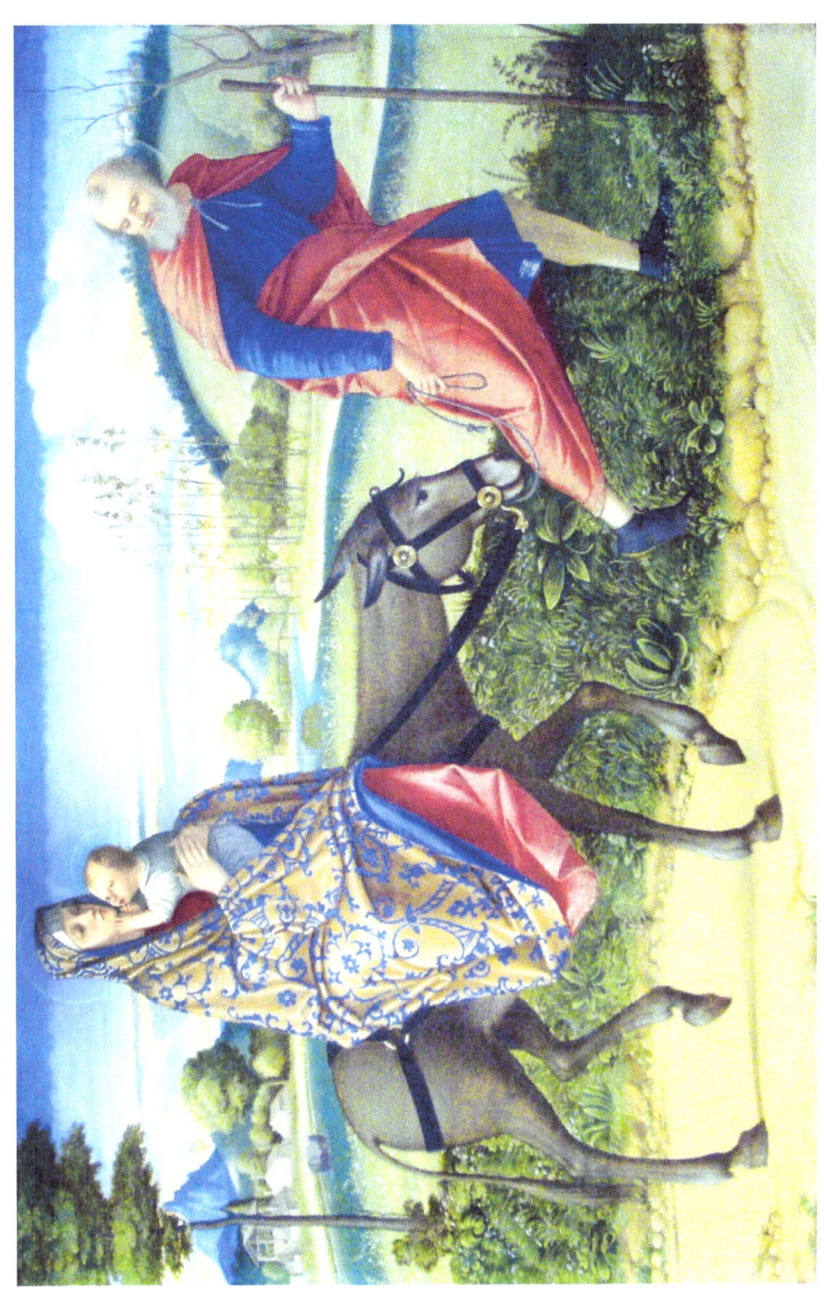

Holy Family with Angels

Artist: Lorenzo Lotto
Date: circa 1536-1537
Media: oil on canvas
Style or Movement: Italian Renaissance
Current location: Louvre Museum, Paris, France
➪

Lorenzo Lotto (about 1480-1556/7) was born in Venice and was influenced by the Venetian painters, but his works remained somewhat apart from the main Venetian tradition. His highly individual style conveys devotion, humanity, and interest in capturing real-life appearances.

The Italian Renaissance was distinct from the Northern Renaissance, which was centered in Eastern Europe and closely linked to the Protestant Reformation. Paintings of this period were detailed and elaborate.

This meticulous execution of the details of this painting show a magnificent intensity of color. The verdant landscape recalls the meeting of the two holy children, John the Baptist and the Infant Jesus. Mary, Joseph, Elizabeth, Zechariah, and angels stand by in wonder and adoration. The divine figures, while realistic, are set apart by the illumination of a bright heavenly light.

Religious significance of the subject matter: The infant Jesus and John the Baptist with family members and angels looking on.

The Bible does not record the families of Jesus and John the Baptist being together aside from the visitation of Mary to Elizabeth while both were still expecting their children. It is very conceivable, though, that these two children did meet during their childhood and play together as depicted in the painting. Elizabeth and Mary were relatives, and it seems likely that they would be very interested in meeting and seeing each other's babies who both had miraculous conceptions.

> At that time Mary got ready and hurried to a town in the hill country of Judea, where she entered Zechariah's home and greeted Elizabeth. When Elizabeth heard Mary's greeting, the baby leaped in her womb, and Elizabeth was filled with the Holy Spirit. In a loud voice she exclaimed: "Blessed are you among women, and blessed is the child you will bear! But why am I so favored, that the mother of my Lord should come to me? As soon as the sound of your greeting reached my ears, the baby in my womb leaped for joy. Blessed is she who has believed that the Lord would fulfill his promises to her!" (Luke 1:39-45)

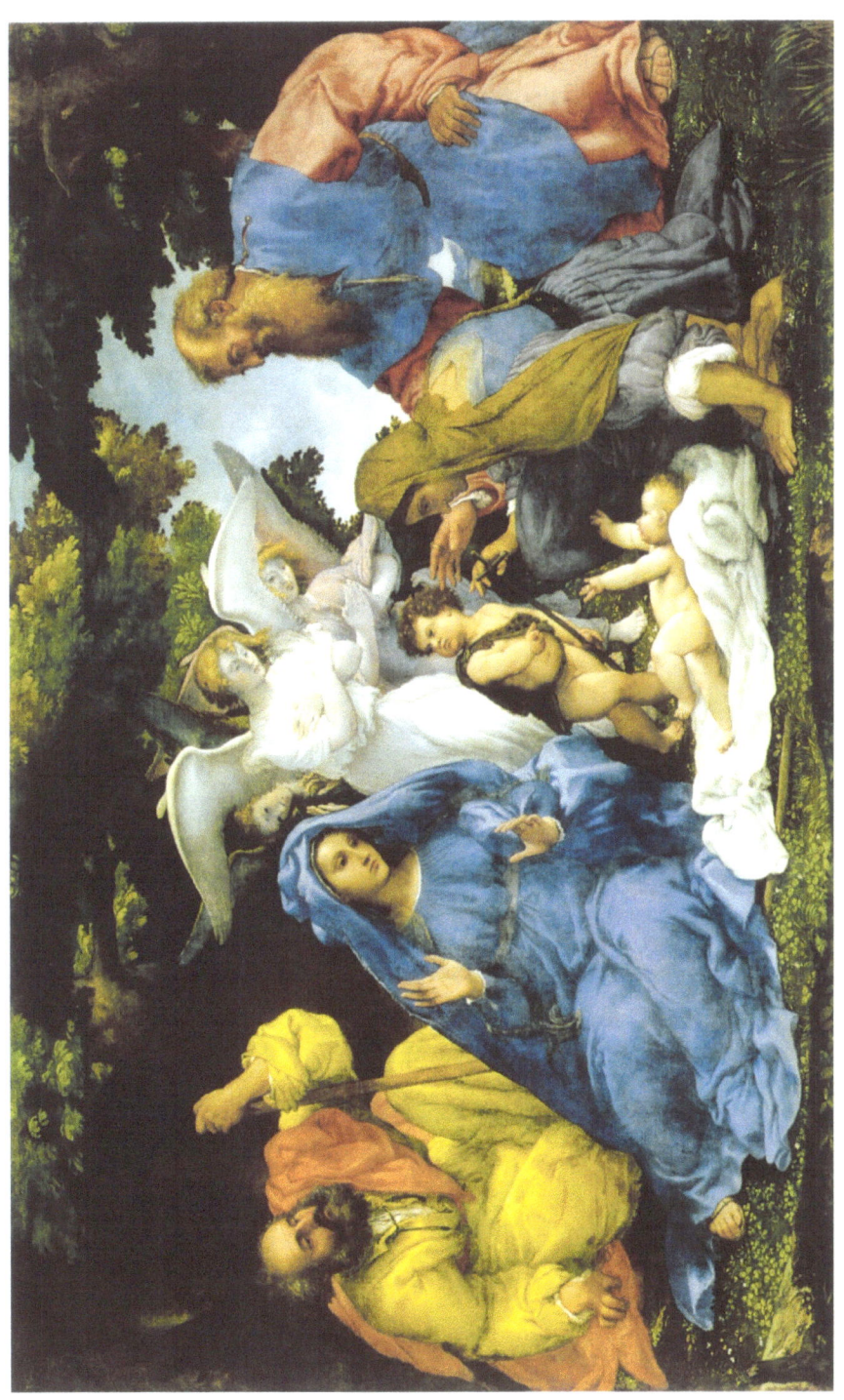

Saint Joseph with the Infant Jesus

Artist: Guido Reni
Date: circa 1635
Media: oil on canvas
Style or Movement: Baroque
Current location: Hermitage Museum, St. Petersburg, Russia
⇨

Guido Reni (1575-1642) was a painter of the High Baroque style, and his techniques were used by the Bolognese school. His religious compositions made him one of the most famous European painters of his time. The mood of his paintings is calm and serene, with a softness of form and color.

Oil painting incorporates pigments with a medium of drying oil used as a binder. Common oils used include linseed, poppy seed, walnut, and safflower oils. The type of oil affects the drying time, sheen, and other effects, such as the ability to create translucence. Oil is slow drying and allows the artist to revise his work.

This painting depicts a tender, loving St. Joseph gazing at the newborn Jesus in wonder and adoration. The figures seem to almost extend out of the canvas. The infant is portrayed in a radiant divine light framed by St. Joseph's orange robe, which is in sharp contrast to the mostly dark background. Jesus appears as if he is almost floating in Joseph's arms.

St. Joseph, who worked as a carpenter, was most likely not as old as he is portrayed in this painting, but it was a custom at the time of this painting to portray Joseph as much older than Mary.

Religious significance of the subject matter: St. Joseph lovingly accepted Jesus and took care of him as if he were his own son.

Very little is recorded of St. Joseph in the Bible, but we do know a few things about him. He was a carpenter by trade. He took Mary as his wife and was a foster father to Jesus. He knew through miraculous dreams and revelations from God that Jesus was the Messiah and Lord. Therefore, it would make sense that St. Joseph not only loved Jesus as a son but also adored him as God. It is probable that he also was humbly amazed and grateful to God that he was chosen to be the foster father of God's only begotten son.

> Now the birth of Jesus Christ was like this; for after his mother, Mary, was engaged to Joseph, before they came together, she was found pregnant by the Holy Spirit. Joseph, her husband, being a righteous man, and not willing to make her a public example, intended to put her away secretly.
> But when he thought about these things, behold, an angel of the Lord appeared to him in a dream, saying, "Joseph, son of David, don't be afraid to take to yourself Mary, your wife, for that which is conceived in her is of the Holy Spirit She shall give birth to a son. You shall call his name Jesus, for it is he who shall save his people from their sins."
> Now all this has happened, that it might be fulfilled which was spoken by the Lord through the prophet, saying, "Behold, the virgin shall be with child, and shall give birth to a son. They shall call his name Immanuel"; which is, being interpreted, "God with us." Joseph arose from his sleep, and did as the angel of the Lord commanded him, and took his wife to himself; and didn't know her sexually until she had given birth to her firstborn son. He named him Jesus. (Matthew 1:18-24)

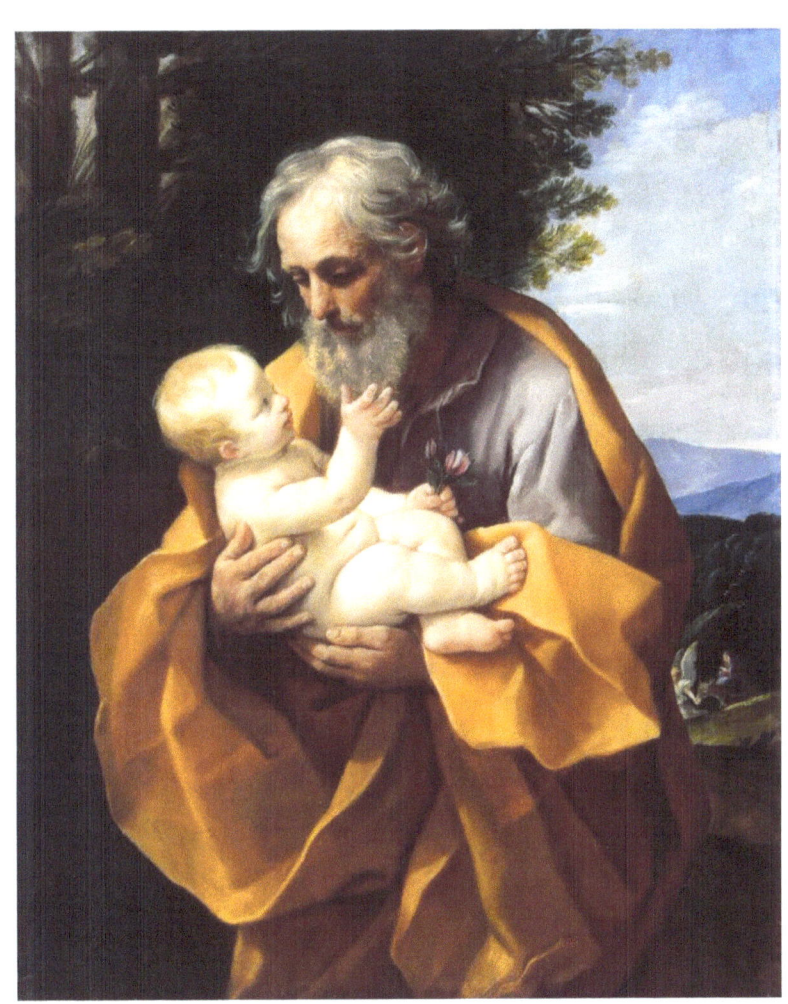

Baptism of Christ

Artist: Pietro Perugino
Date: circa 1482
Media: Fresco
Style or Movement: Italian Renaissance
Current location: Sistine Chapel, Vatican City
⇨

Pietro Perugino was one of the earliest Italian artists to master the technique of oil painting. He mainly worked in Florence; however, he took a journey to Rome in 1480 to work on the Sistine Chapel frescos.

The fresco technique was popular during the Renaissance. It consists of using a brush to paint onto a layer of fresh plaster made of wet lime. The pigments then were allowed to dry directly on the plaster allowing for a greater permanency. This method only allowed the artist several hours to make changes and complete the artwork before the plaster dried.

This huge fresco (about 11 x 15 feet) is likely the combined effort of Perugino and his assistant Pinturicchio, who probably did the landscape and scenery. In the center John is baptizing Jesus in the River Jordan. The Holy Spirit in the form of a dove, sent by God the Father who is surrounded by angels, descends from the sky. On the sides Christ is preaching on the right and the John the Baptist on the left. The fresco is almost symmetrical and rich in symbolism.

Religious significance of the subject matter: John the Baptist baptizes Jesus.

Jesus received the baptism of repentance even though he was without sin "for this is the fitting way for us to fulfill all righteousness". The occasion also reveals the Trinitarian nature of God to all future generations.

> Then Jesus came from Galilee to the Jordan to John, to be baptized by him. But John would have hindered him, saying, "I need to be baptized by you, and you come to me?" But Jesus, answering, said to him, "Allow it now, for this is the fitting way for us to fulfill all righteousness." Then he allowed him. Jesus, when he was baptized, went up directly from the water: and behold, the heavens were opened to him. He saw the Spirit of God descending as a dove, and coming on him. Behold, a voice out of the heavens said, "This is my beloved Son, with whom I am well pleased." (Matthew 3:13-17)

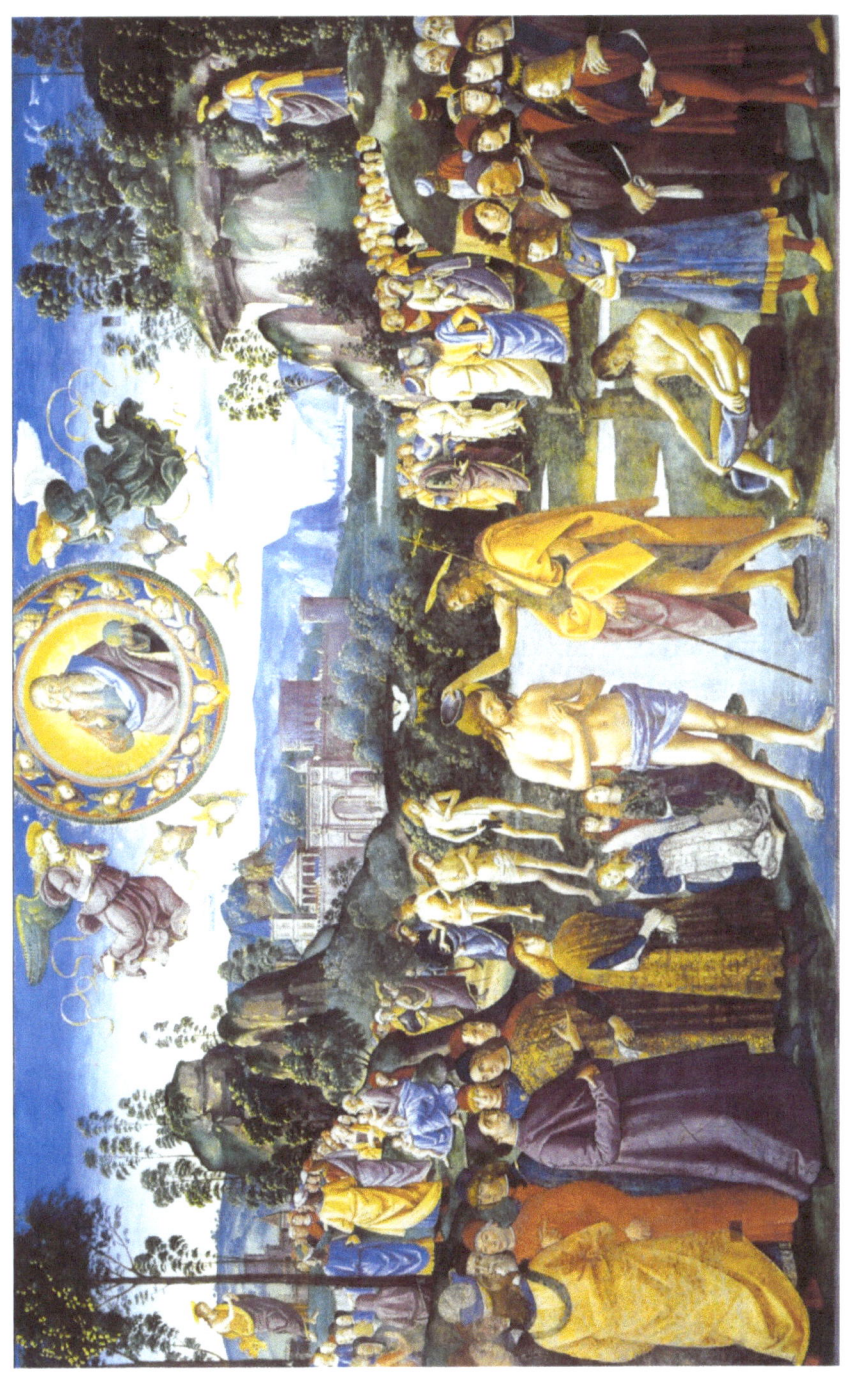

The Return of the Prodigal Son

Artist: Bartolome Esteban Murillo
Date: circa 1667-1670
Media: oil on canvas
Style or Movement: Baroque
Current location: National Gallery of Art, Washington DC
⇨

Bartolomé Esteban Murillo (1618-1682), a leading Spanish Baroque artist, is best known for his religious works. He also painted realistic depictions of the everyday life of his times, in which he used the contrast of light and shade to produce soft forms of rich color.

The use of canvas in oil painting allows for easier transport than paintings done on wood because canvas is lighter. The standard for the canvas is a strong and durable linen, which is cut and stretched over a frame and secured by tacks. Cotton, which is less expensive, is also used and can be stretched very tightly.

This painting emphasizes the protective embrace of the loving father as he welcomes his son home. The clothes held by the servant represent the work of mercy of clothing the naked. The neutral background of misty clouds and soft figures are in sharp contrast to the warm bright colors of the central figures.

Religious significance of the subject matter: God's great mercy and love

This story of the Prodigal Son told by Jesus demonstrates God's great mercy and love for his children. It shows how God awaits all sinners to return to him and rejoices at their return.

> He said, "A certain man had two sons. The younger of them said to his father, 'Father, give me my share of your property.' He divided his livelihood between them. Not many days after, the younger son gathered all of this together and traveled into a far country. There he wasted his property with riotous living. When he had spent all of it, there arose a severe famine in that country, and he began to be in need. He went and joined himself to one of the citizens of that country, and he sent him into his fields to feed pigs. He wanted to fill his belly with the husks that the pigs ate, but no one gave him any. But when he came to himself he said, 'How many hired servants of my father's have bread enough to spare, and I'm dying with hunger! I will get up and go to my father, and will tell him, "Father, I have sinned against heaven, and in your sight. I am no more worthy to be called your son. Make me as one of your hired servants.'"
>
> "He arose, and came to his father. But while he was still far off, his father saw him, and was moved with compassion, and ran, and fell on his neck, and kissed him. The son said to him, 'Father, I have sinned against heaven, and in your sight. I am no longer worthy to be called your son.'
>
> "But the father said to his servants, 'Bring out the best robe, and put it on him. Put a ring on his hand, and shoes on his feet. Bring the fattened calf, kill it, and let us eat, and celebrate; for this, my son, was dead, and is alive again. He was lost, and is found.' They began to celebrate.
>
> "Now his elder son was in the field. As he came near to the house, he heard music and dancing. He called one of the servants to him, and asked what was going on. He said to him, 'Your brother has come, and your father has killed the fattened calf, because he has received him back safe and healthy.' But he was angry, and would not go in. Therefore his father came out, and begged him. But he answered his father, 'Behold, these many years I have served you, and I never disobeyed a commandment of yours, but you never gave me a goat that I might celebrate with my friends. But when this, your son, came, who has devoured your living with prostitutes, you killed the fattened calf for him.'
>
> "He said to him, 'Son, you are always with me, and all that is mine is yours.'" (Luke 15:11-31)

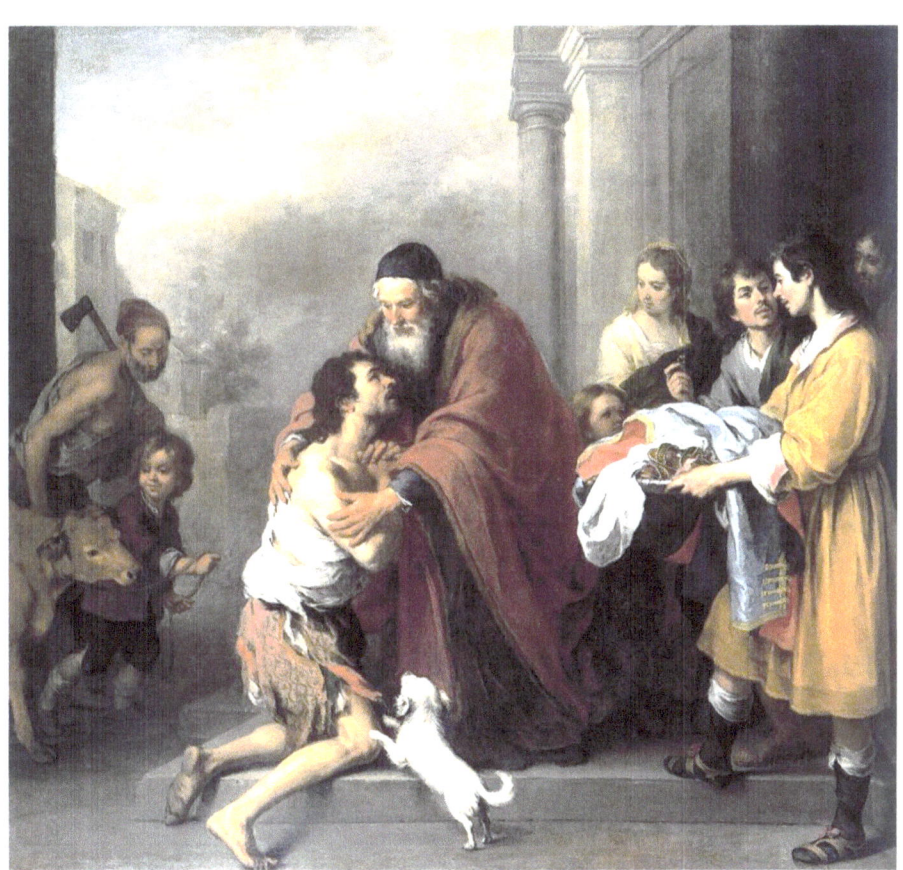

Christ in the Storm on the Sea of Galilee

Artist: Rembrandt
Date: 1633
Media: oil on canvas
Style or Movement: Dutch Golden Age
Current Location: unknown. It was historically located in the Dutch Room at the Isabella Stewart Gardner Museum, Boston, MA
⇨

Rembrandt van Rijn (1601-1669) is usually regarded as the greatest artist of Holland's Golden Age. He was a prolific painter, etcher, and draftsman. He was highly successful and many imitations of his work were made in later periods.

The Dutch Golden Age spanned roughly the 17th century in which Dutch art was among the most acclaimed in the world. Dutch Golden Age paintings followed many of the tendencies of the Baroque, but the movement was the leader in still life, landscape, and genre painting.

This painting was stolen, along with twelve others, in 1990 by thieves disguised as police officers and has never been found. The painting depicts a dangerous spectacle of dark, churning seas and blackening sky perhaps symbolizing the darkness of sin. The eye is automatically drawn to the dazzling light, perhaps symbolizing redemption, surrounding and engulfing the terrified disciples as they wait for Christ to save them.

Religious significance of the subject matter: Jesus calms the storm to the amazement of his disciples.

Jesus worked many miracles to demonstrate that he was the Son of God. One of these miracles demonstrated his power over the weather. Many came to believe that Jesus was God and the promised Messiah because of the miracles he performed.

> Now on one of those days, he entered into a boat, himself and his disciples, and he said to them, "Let's go over to the other side of the lake." So they launched out. But as they sailed, he fell asleep. A wind storm came down on the lake, and they were taking on dangerous amounts of water. They came to him, and awoke him, saying, "Master, master, we are dying!" He awoke, and rebuked the wind and the raging of the water, and they ceased, and it was calm. He said to them, "Where is your faith?" Being afraid they marveled, saying to one another, "Who is this, then, that he commands even the winds and the water, and they obey him?" They arrived at the country of the Gadarenes, which is opposite Galilee. (Luke 8:22-26)

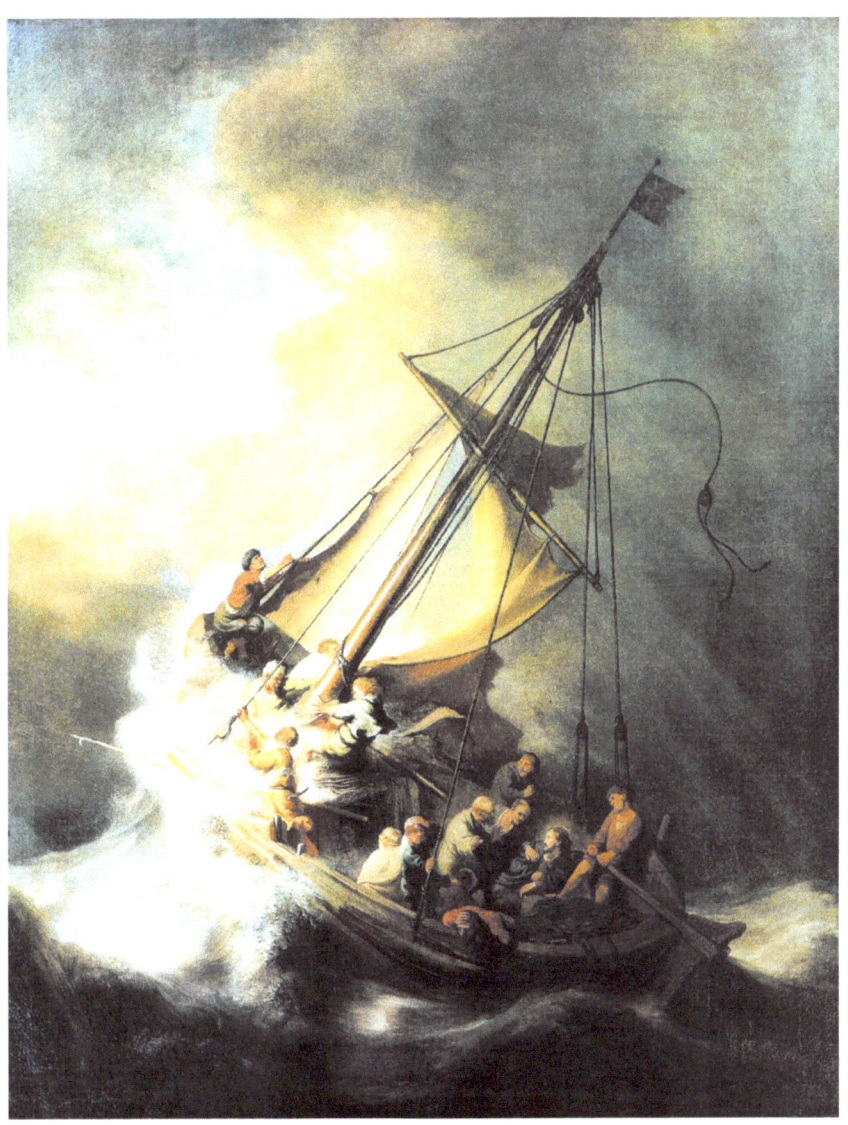

Miraculous Draught of Fishes

Artist: Raphael
Date: 1515-16
Media: Tempera on paper, mounted on canvas
Style or Movement: High Renaissance
Current Location: Victoria and Albert Museum, London, England

Raffaello Sanzio da Urbino (1483 –1520) was an Italian painter and architect of the High Renaissance period. Along with Michelangelo and Leonardo da Vinci, he is considered one of the three greatest artists of that period. He produced a large number of works even though he died at only 37 years of age. Many of his frescos are at the Vatican Palace.

The Raphael Cartoons are seven large cartoons that were drawings for tapestries and showed scenes from the Gospels and Acts of the Apostles. The Miraculous Draught of Fishes was one of Raphael's cartoons. The cartoons were painted in a glue distemper medium on many sheets of paper glued together (as can be seen in the full-size illustrations) and later mounted on a canvas backing.

This cartoon shows Jesus in a glowing garment and the muscular disciples bathed in the bright light of the miracle at dawn. Birds emerge from the background and are drawn to the scene. The lake reflects the action and intensity of the disciples as they work.

Religious significance of the subject matter: Jesus performs a miracle where the apostles catch a very large number of fish.

> After these things, Jesus revealed himself again to the disciples at the sea of Tiberias. He revealed himself this way. Simon Peter, Thomas called Didymus, Nathanael of Cana in Galilee, and the sons of Zebedee, and two others of his disciples were together. Simon Peter said to them, "I'm going fishing."
> They told him, "We are also coming with you." They immediately went out, and entered into the boat. That night, they caught nothing. But when day had already come, Jesus stood on the beach, yet the disciples didn't know that it was Jesus.
> Jesus therefore said to them, "Children, have you anything to eat?"
> They answered him, "No."
> He said to them, "Cast the net on the right side of the boat, and you will find some."
> They cast it therefore, and now they weren't able to draw it in for the multitude of fish. That disciple therefore whom Jesus loved said to Peter, "It's the Lord!" (Luke 21:1-7)

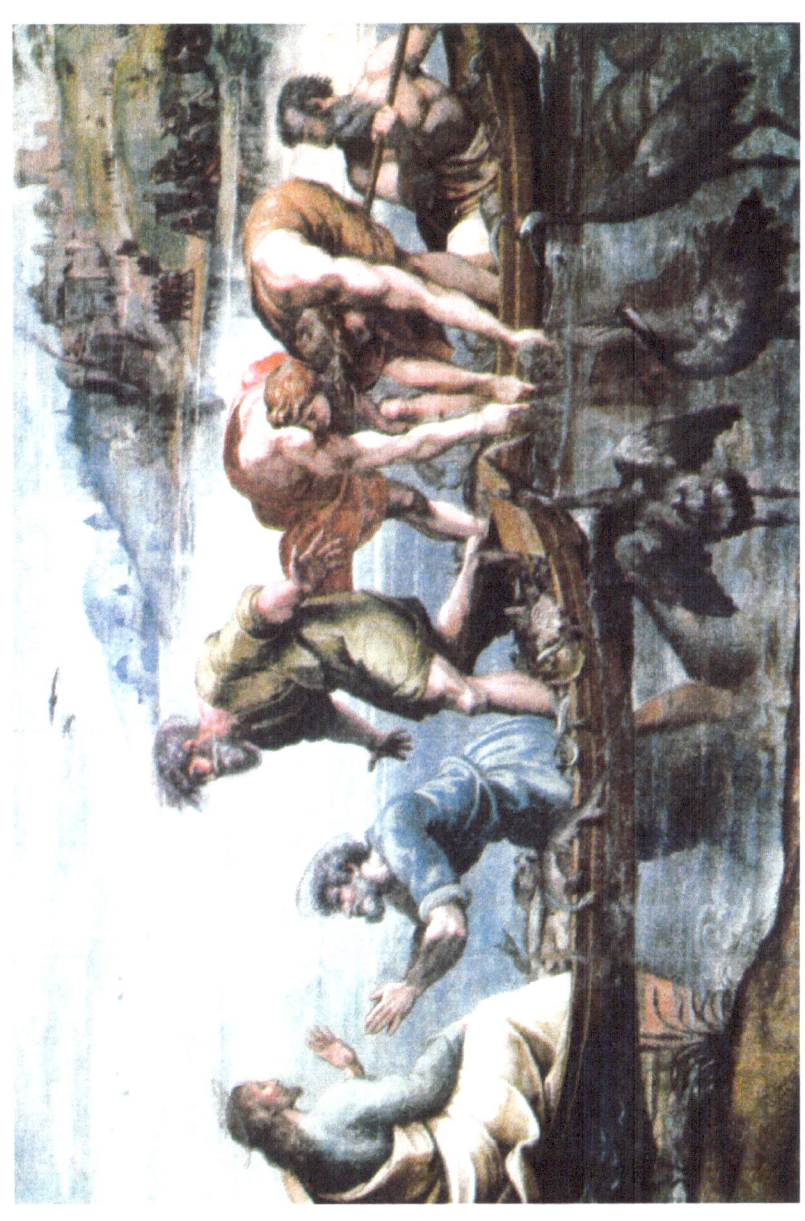

The Last Supper

Artist: Leonardo da Vinci
Date: 1495-1498
Media: oil and tempera on plaster
Style or Movement: High Renaissance
Current location: Santa Maria delle Grazie, Milan
⇨

Leonardo da Vinci (1452-1519) was an Italian painter, architect, draftsman, sculptor, engineer, inventor, writer, and scientist. He was one of the greatest minds of the Italian Renaissance and one of the greatest painters of all time.

The Last Supper was painted on dry wall rather than wet plaster so is not a true fresco. Leonardo sealed the stone wall with a double layer of plaster, then added an undercoat of white lead to enhance the brightness of the oil and tempera. In this way he attempted to create greater detail and luminosity than can be achieved with traditional fresco. Soon after the painting was completed, it began to deteriorate. The effects of humidity on the thin exterior wall did not allow the paint to properly adhere to the wall.

This painting shows the last supper of Jesus with his twelve apostles. The apostles show different reactions to the news from Jesus that he will be betrayed. Leonardo's notebook, which was found in the 19th century, identified the location of the apostles in the painting. From left to right the first group of three apostles are Bartholomew, James, and Andrew, who are all surprised. Next is Judas Iscariot (with his elbow on the table) in the shadows perhaps because of shame, with Peter, who appears angry, and John who appears to faint. Jesus is in the center. On his right are another group of three who are Thomas who seems upset, James the Greater who looks stunned, and Philip, perhaps waiting for more explanation. The last are Matthew and Jude Thaddeus, who seem to be questioning Simon on the far right.

Religious significance of the subject matter: The Last Supper of Christ

> Now on the first day of unleavened bread, the disciples came to Jesus, saying to him, "Where do you want us to prepare for you to eat the Passover?"
> He said, "Go into the city to a certain person, and tell him, 'The Teacher says, "My time is at hand. I will keep the Passover at your house with my disciples." ' "
> The disciples did as Jesus commanded them, and they prepared the Passover. Now when evening had come, he was reclining at the table with the twelve disciples. As they were eating, he said, "Most certainly I tell you that one of you will betray me."
> They were exceedingly sorrowful, and each began to ask him, "It isn't me, is it, Lord?"
> He answered, "He who dipped his hand with me in the dish, the same will betray me. The Son of Man goes, even as it is written of him, but woe to that man through whom the Son of Man is betrayed! It would be better for that man if he had not been born."
> Judas, who betrayed him, answered, "It isn't me, is it, Rabbi?"
> He said to him, "You said it."
> As they were eating, Jesus took bread, blessed it, and broke it. He gave to the disciples, and said, "Take, eat; this is my body." He took the cup, gave thanks, and gave to them, saying, "All of you drink it, for this is my blood of the new covenant, which is poured out for many for the remission of sins. But I tell you that I will not drink of this fruit of the vine from now on, until that day when I drink it anew with you in my Father's Kingdom."
> When they had sung a hymn, they went out to the Mount of Olives. (Matthew 26:17-30)

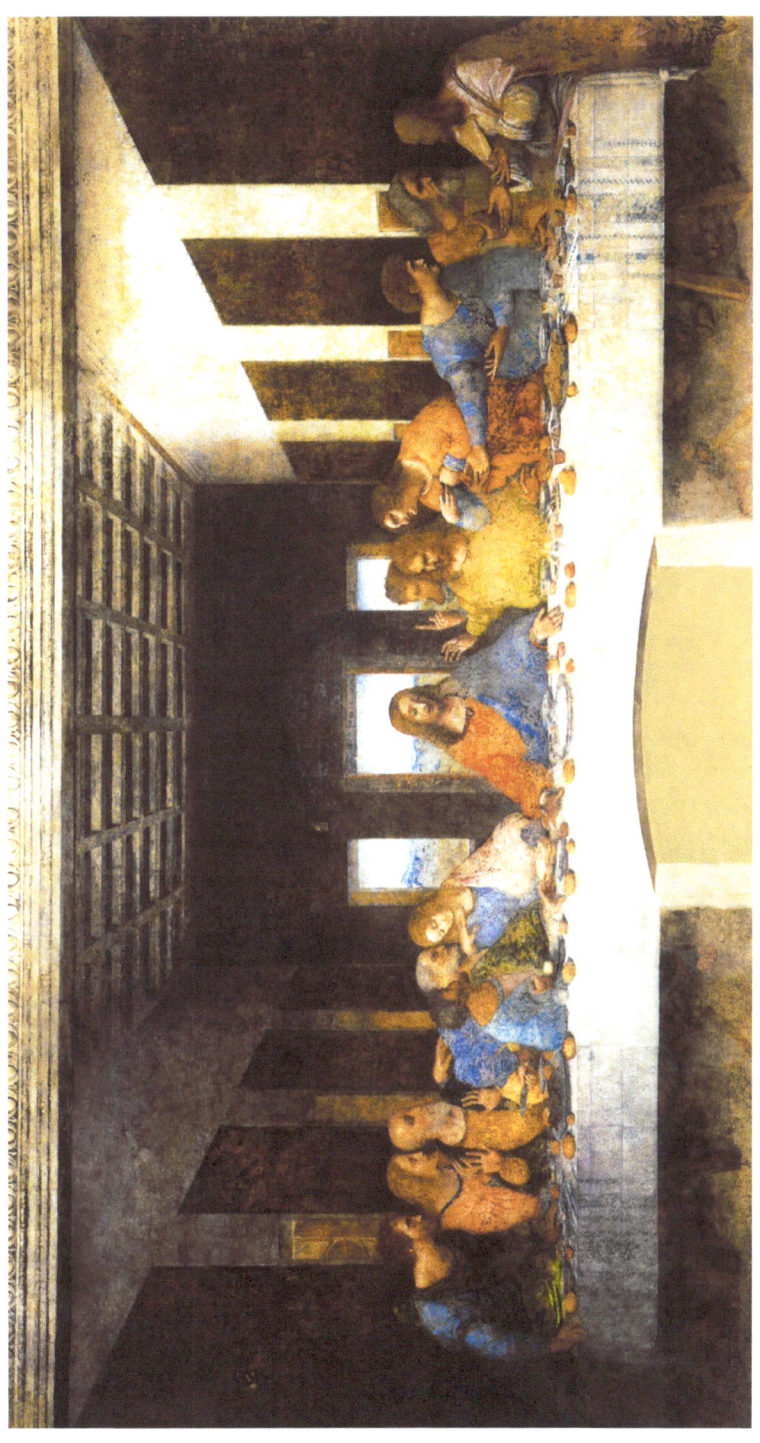

Christ Carrying the Cross

Artist: Lorenzo Lotto
Date: 1526
Media: oil on canvas
Style or Movement: High Renaissance
Current location: Louvre Museum, Paris France

Lorenzo Lotto (about 1480-1556/7) was born in Venice and was influenced by the Venetian painters, but his works remained somewhat apart from the main Venetian tradition. His highly individual style conveys devotion, humanity, and more interest in capturing real-life appearances.

The High Renaissance is the period denoting the culmination or highest point of the Italian Renaissance dating from the 1490s to around 1527.

This painting is virtually square. The scene is entirely on Christ who wears a blood-red cloak that symbolizes the Passion. Christ is being struck on all sides as his shoulders and head are dramatically pressed forward towards the viewer. His countenance seems to portray love, knowledge, and acceptance, perhaps of his Father's will and those he came to save.

Religious significance of the subject matter: Jesus carries the cross to his own crucifixion and death.

Christians believe that Jesus died for our sins so that we might be saved and have eternal life and happiness.

> So then he delivered him to them to be crucified. So they took Jesus and led him away. He went out, bearing his cross, to the place called "The Place of a Skull," which is called in Hebrew, "Golgotha," where they crucified him, and with him two others, on either side one, and Jesus in the middle. Pilate wrote a title also, and put it on the cross. There was written, "JESUS OF NAZARETH, THE KING OF THE JEWS." Therefore many of the Jews read this title, for the place where Jesus was crucified was near the city; and it was written in Hebrew, in Latin, and in Greek. (John 19:16-20)

> Now I declare to you, brothers, the Good News which I preached to you, which also you received, in which you also stand, by which also you are saved, if you hold firmly the word which I preached to you—unless you believed in vain. For I delivered to you first of all that which I also received: that Christ died for our sins according to the Scriptures . . . (1 Corinthians 15:1-4)

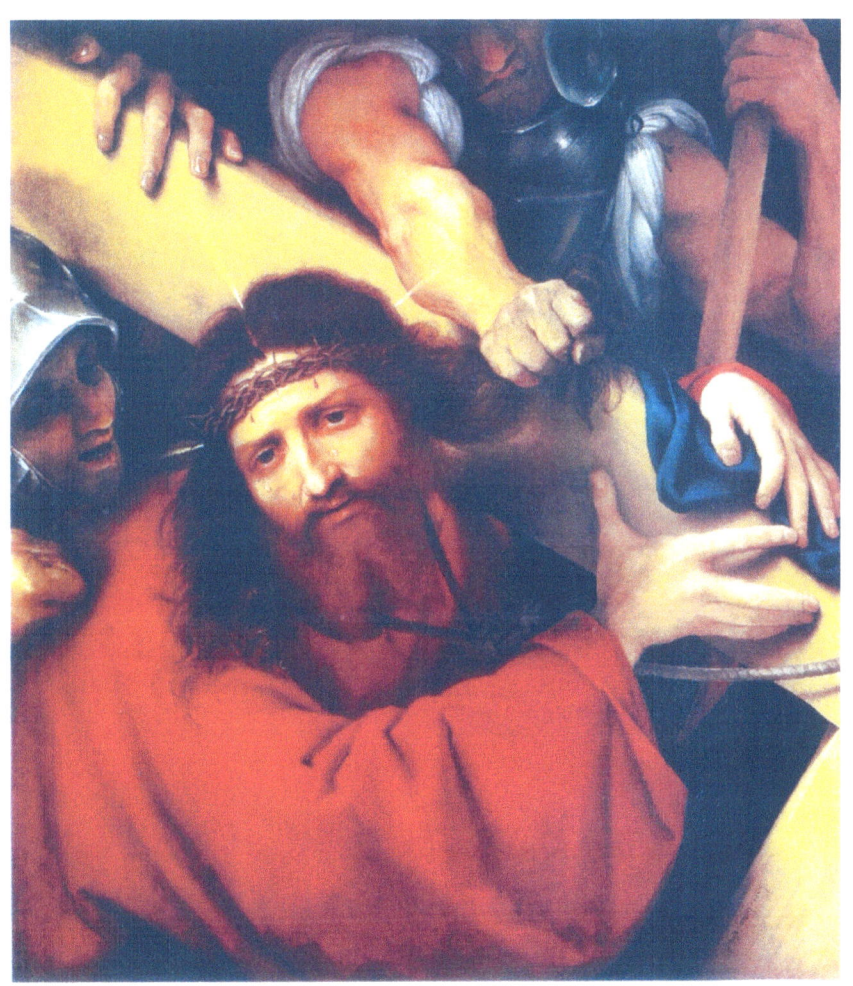

Christ Falls on the Route to Calvary

Artist: Raphael
Date: 1515-16
Media: oil on panel transferred to canvas
Style or Movement: High Renaissance
Current location: Museo Del Prado, Madrid, Spain

Raffaello Sanzio da Urbino (1483 –1520), known as Raphael, was an Italian painter and architect of the High Renaissance. Raphael was enormously productive even though he died at the early age of 37. Many of his works are found in the Vatican Palace, where the frescoed Raphael Rooms were the central and largest work of his career. He was extremely influential during his lifetime.

Paintings done on a wood panel decay over time, and the wood may also crack or distort. This painting was done on a wood panel and then later transferred to canvas to help preserve it. This type of preservation began in the 18th century and was widely practiced in the second half of the 19th century. Today there are improved methods of wood preservation.

Warm coloring is used in the painting, which depicts varying emotions from the suffering Mother Mary and other holy women to the mixed emotions of the crowd and cruelty of the soldiers. Jesus tenderly looks at his mother in his anguish. This painting has many devotional elements of the Stations of the Cross calling to mind what Jesus underwent including falling while carrying the cross, meeting his sorrowful mother, and Simon of Cyrene helping him to carry his cross.

Religious significance of the subject matter: Christ falls while carrying his cross.

Jesus suffered and died for our sins because of his great love for us. The Stations of the Cross (also called the Way of the Cross) is a devotion that can be found in many Catholic parishes as well as a number of Anglican, Lutheran, and Methodist parishes. The Stations of the Cross devotion is similar to a spiritual pilgrimage where one typically stops at each image or station to pray and reflect on an event from the passion and death of the Lord Jesus Christ.

The traditional fourteen Stations of the Cross are as follows:

1 - Jesus is condemned to death.
2 - Jesus carries his cross.
3 - Jesus falls the first time.
4 - Jesus meets his mother.
5 - Simon of Cyrene helps Jesus carry the cross.
6 - Veronica wipes the face of Jesus.
7 - Jesus falls the second time.
8 - Jesus meets the women of Jerusalem.
9 - Jesus falls the third time.
10 - Jesus is stripped of his garments.
11 - Jesus is nailed to the cross.
12 - Jesus dies on the cross.
13 - Jesus is taken down from the cross.
14 - Jesus is laid in the tomb.

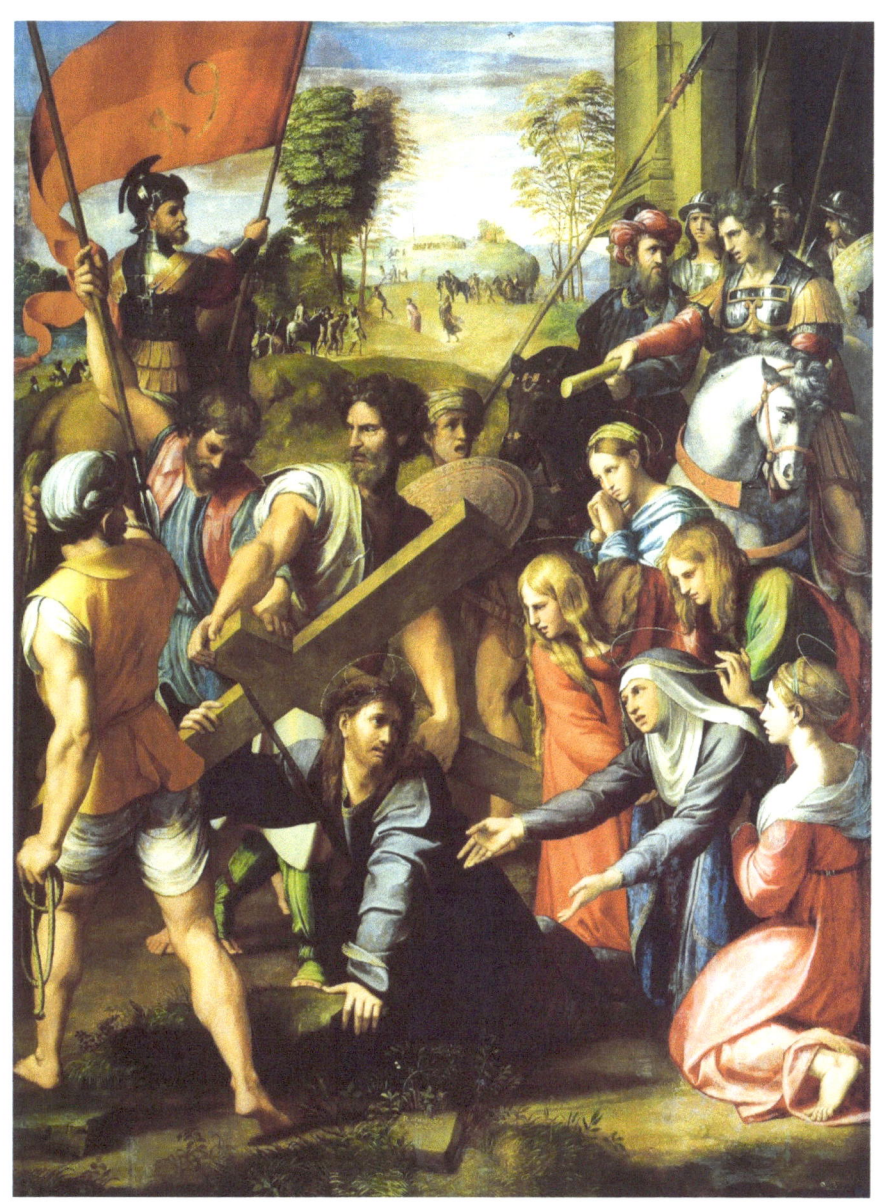

Pietà

Artist: Michelangelo
Date: 1498-1499
Media: Marble
Style or Movement: Italian Renaissance
Current location: St. Peter's Basilica, Vatican City
⇨

Michelangelo di Lodovico Buonarroti Simoni (1475–1564) envisioned that the subject matter of the sculpture already existed within the marble, and his desire was to set it free. He considered himself primarily as a sculptor, and he was a genius in portraying the human form.

Marble is a metamorphic rock derived from limestone. Marble has a slight translucency that it not commonly available in other stones, and the subsurface scattering of light can be comparable to human skin. It is also relatively soft and easy to work and polish when it is first cut from the quarry. Marble becomes harder and more durable with age.

This Pietà statue sculpted from marble shows the Virgin Mary holding the lifeless body of her son Jesus. Mary appears youthful and radiates an inner beauty and strength. Sculpted from marble this sculpture balances Renaissance ideals with the classical beauty of Naturalism, and it established Michelangelo as the greatest sculptor of his time. This is the only sculpture that Michelangelo ever signed due to overhearing visitors who thought that it had been sculpted by his competitor. He carved his signature into the sash on Mary's breast.

Religious significance of the subject matter: Mary's sorrow as she holds Jesus's lifeless body in her arms

One can only imagine the depth of Mary's sorrow at the suffering and death of her son. One title of Mary is Our Lady of Sorrows. Yet we can also imagine that she was comforted by her perfect faith and by the knowledge that Jesus was the Son of God and therefore was alive in spirit even though his body had died. She knew that Jesus would rise again in three days, and therefore even though sorrowful, she was also filled with hope.

> Joseph and his mother were marveling at the things which were spoken concerning him, and Simeon blessed them, and said to Mary, his mother, "Behold, this child is set for the falling and the rising of many in Israel, and for a sign which is spoken against. Yes, a sword will pierce through your own soul, that the thoughts of many hearts may be revealed" (Luke 2:33-35).

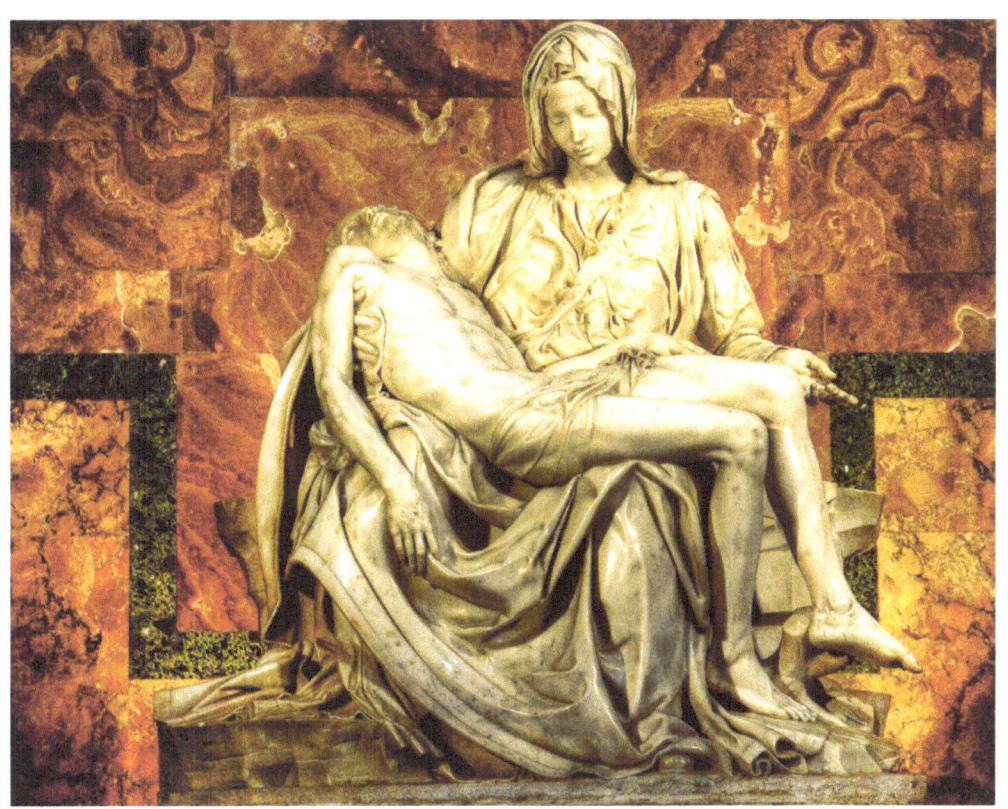

Assumption of the Virgin Mary

Artist: Guido Reni
Date: 1642
Media: silk
Style or Movement: Baroque
Current location: Alte Pinakothek, Munich, Germany
⇨

Guido Reni (1575-1642) was a painter of the High Baroque style whose paintings were noted for their classical idealism and harmony with a preference for gracefully posed figures. His inspirations mainly came ancient Greek sculptures from the frescoes of Raphael. Pope Paul V commissioned him for many important works, and he painted many frescos in chapels.

In this painting Mary, the radiant Mother of God, is being lifted body and soul into heaven by a multitude of angels. The divine heavens above are bright, open, and clear, while below it is cloudy, dark, and dreary. The glorious blue garment is striking as it frames her perfect pose of humility and grace as she expectantly waits to meet her son in glory.

Religious significance of the subject matter: Assumption of Mary into Heaven

The Assumption of the Mary refers to the body of Mary being taken up into heaven at the end of her life rather than being subject to decay. The resurrection of Jesus Christ's body as well as the assumption of Mary's body into Heaven are significant events that remind us that human beings are born with an immortal soul that never dies and a body that, while subject to death here on earth, will also rise on the last day.

> Most certainly I tell you, he who hears my word, and believes him who sent me, has eternal life, and doesn't come into judgment, but has passed out of death into life. Most certainly, I tell you, the hour comes, and now is, when the dead will hear the Son of God's voice; and those who hear will live. For as the Father has life in himself, even so he gave to the Son also to have life in himself. He also gave him authority to execute judgment, because he is a son of man. Don't marvel at this, for the hour comes, in which all that are in the tombs will hear his voice, and will come out; those who have done good, to the resurrection of life; and those who have done evil, to the resurrection of judgment. (John 5:24-29)

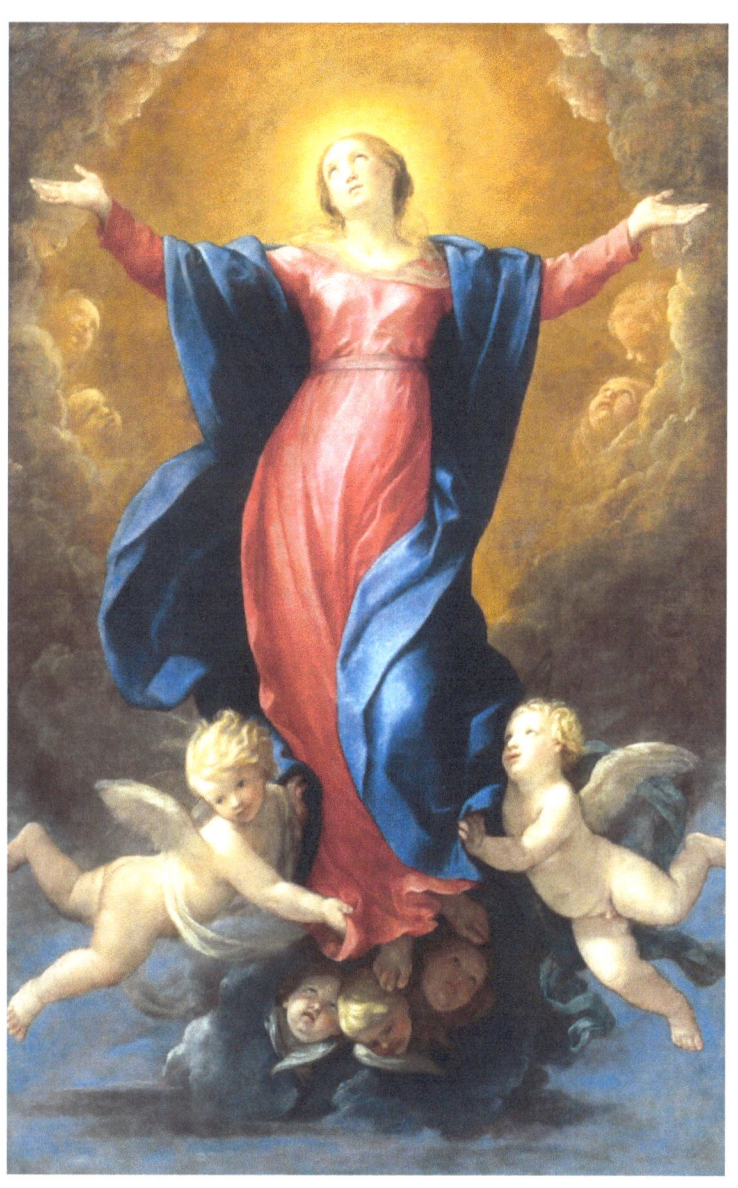

Saint Francis of Assisi Receiving the Stigmata

Artist: Giotto
Date: 1295-1300
Media: tempura on panel
Style or Movement: Proto Renaissance
Current location: Louvre Museum, Paris, France
⇨

Giotto di Bondone (1266/7–1337) was an Italian painter and architect from Florence, Italy. He lived just prior to the Renaissance and was considered one of the first of great artists who contributed to new movements in art seen in the Renaissance. Departing from the Byzantine style, he drew more in accord with nature for a more accurate representation of his subject matter than was currently popular.

The Proto Renaissance period in art was the pre-Renaissance period in Italy in the 14th century. Artists such as Giotto began using a new form of realism, which was further developed during the Renaissance.

This painting shows St. Francis kneeling with open arms gazing at an angel, who appears as if crucified. The unworldly angel is highly symbolic and very different from the usual artistic angelic depiction. The rays from the angel seem to strike St. Francis with a great force as he reacts in surprise and awe. The gold circular halos around the heads of St. Francis and the angel denote holiness.

Religious significance of the subject matter: St. Francis of Assisi receives the stigmata.

St. Francis received the stigmata on a journey when a six-winged angel appeared to him while he prayed. The angel appeared as though crucified, and St. Francis experienced elation joined with pain. The angel left wounds in the saint's hands, feet, and side similar to the wounds of Christ.

Stigmata is a term used to describe marks, wounds, or feelings of pain that appear miraculously in locations similar to the wounds that Christ received during his crucifixion. St. Francis is the first recorded person to receive the stigmata in 1224, even though St. Paul may possibly have had the stigmata as he said, "From now on, let no one cause me any trouble, for I bear the marks of the Lord Jesus branded on my body" (Galatians 6:7). St. Padre Pio of Pietrelcina is a modern-day stigmatist who had the stigmata for over fifty years, which were examined by several physicians.

God as the creator of nature is not limited to the natural laws that he made. Miracles are an event that cannot be explained by natural laws or science. One reason miracles are significant is that they show that there is more than the physical universe and natural laws that we observe; they point to existence of something or someone beyond nature, to the existence of God and his continued involvement with us here on earth.

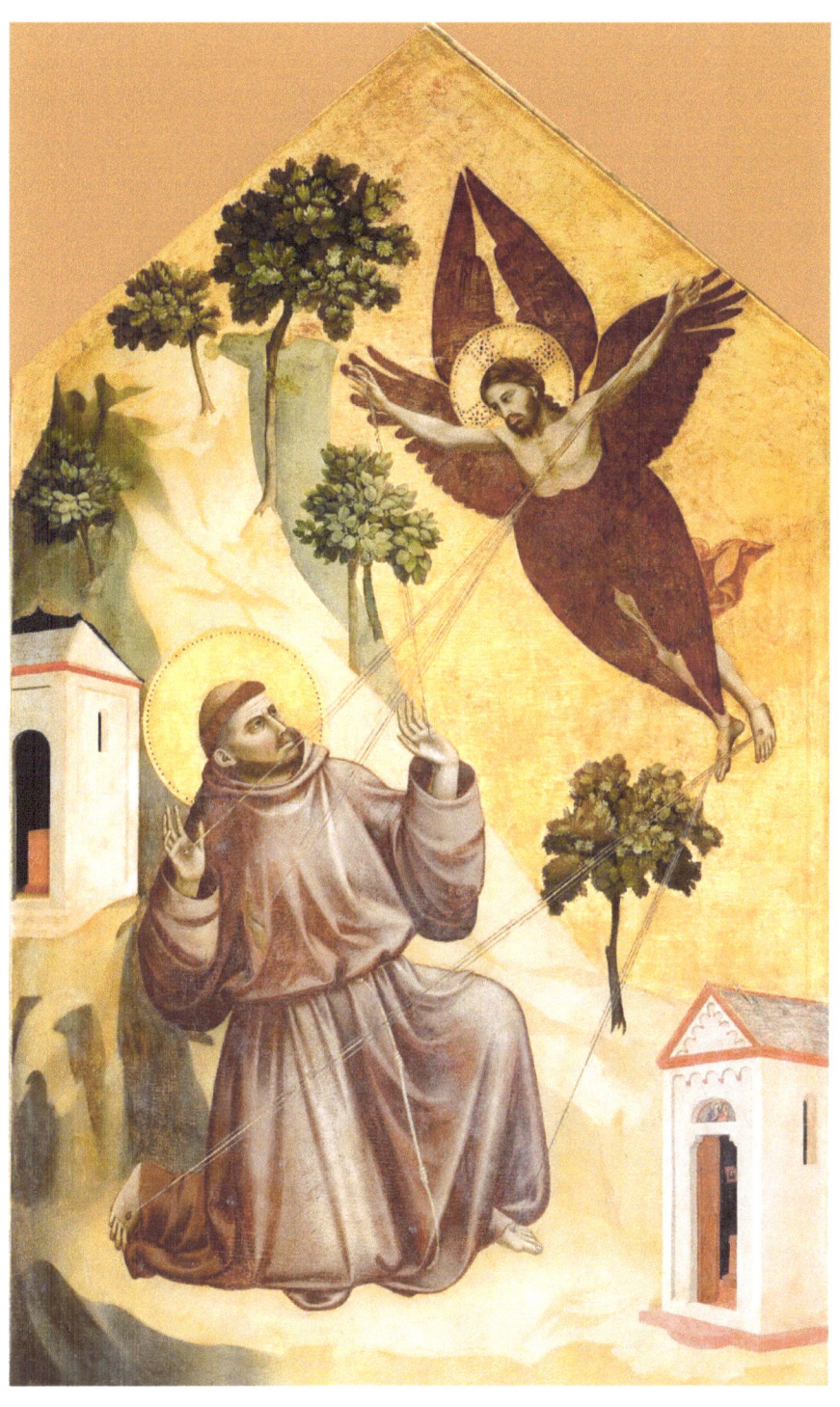

Saint George and the Dragon

Artist: Gustave Moreau
Date: circa 1889-90
Media: oil on canvas
Style or Movement: Symbolism
Current Location: The National Gallery, London, England
⇨

Gustave Moreau (1826 –1898) was a French Symbolist painter and professor who mainly chose biblical and mythological figures for his paintings. Moreau produced more than 8,000 paintings, watercolors, and drawings during his lifetime, many of which are on display in Paris' Musée national Gustave Moreau. The museum is in his former workshop.

Symbolism in art in the latter nineteenth century was a revival of mystical tendencies seen in the Romantic tradition. It often used personal, ambiguous, and obscure imagery from dreams and mythology.

This painting uses dramatic colors and imagery in an attempt to convey the mystical quality of the miraculous story it visually portrays. The subdued princess (upper right background) dressed in her bridal gown seems to be praying as she awaits death above the lake while the defiant St. George wounds the evil dragon with his lance to save her life. St. George's black armor is in sharp contrast to his brilliant horse, glowing halo, and the fabric that depicts the motion of the scene.

Religious significance of the subject matter: St. George slays the dragon to save the princess.

St. George lived in the third century. He was a Roman solider who was martyred under the rule of Diocletian for not renouncing his Christian faith. He is the patron saint of England. While he is a highly venerated saint, it is sometimes difficult to sort out the actual details of the events of his life from the legends that grew up around his great deeds.

The Golden Legend recounts the story of how St. George killed a dragon that harassed and poisoned the city of Silene in the province of Libya. To appease the dragon the people fed the dragon two sheep every day. When they ran out of sheep, they started feeding their children to the dragon, who were chosen by lottery. When the king's daughter was chosen, he offered half of his kingdom and riches if the people would spare his daughter, but they refused.

The princess was dressed like a bride and set out by the lake for the dragon to eat. The legend says that St. George by chance rode by the princess, and heard what had happened. When the dragon came up out of the lake for the princess, St. George prayed and then attacked the dragon with his lance. He seriously wounded and captured it, tying the princess's belt around its neck. Then he and the princess led the dragon back to the city. The people were afraid and ran away. St. George promised to slay the dragon if the city converted to Christianity. They agreed and were baptized. St. George killed the dragon, and the king built a church at the site in which a miraculous spring of water flowed that healed sick people who drank from it.

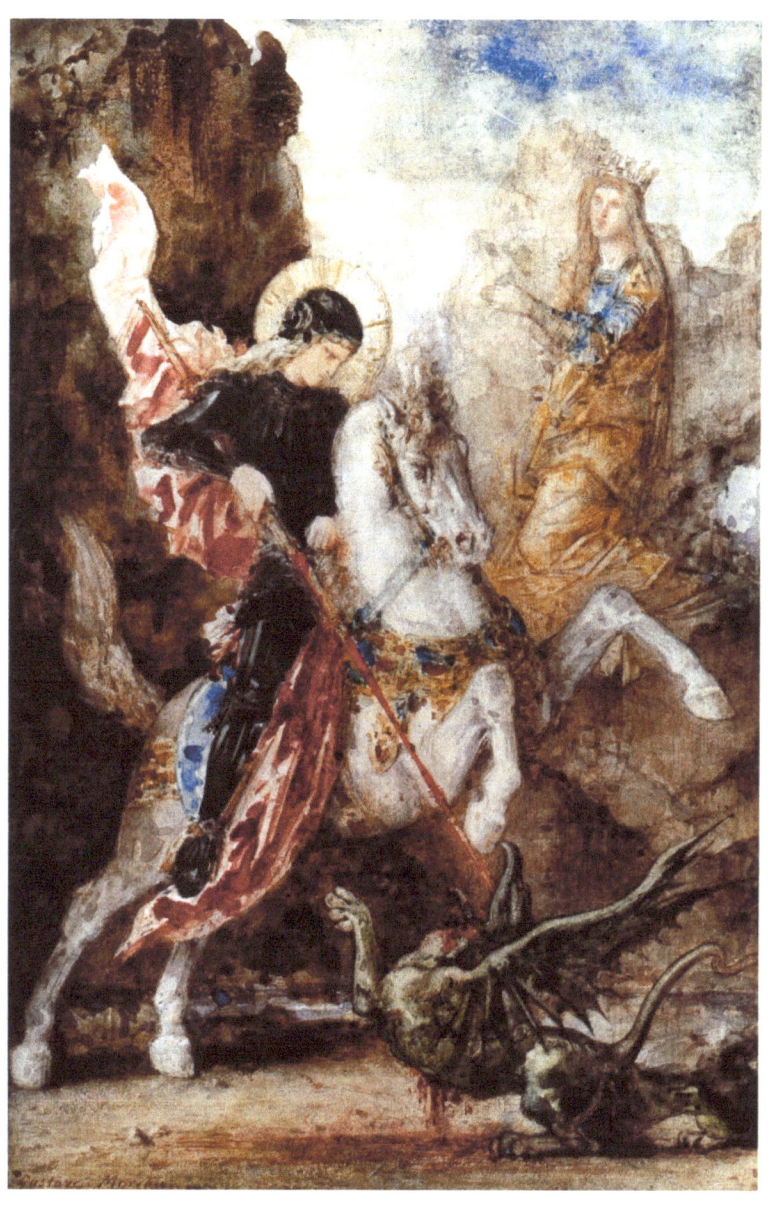

Saint Anthony Preaching to the Fish

Artist: Arnold Böcklin
Date: 1892
Media: oil on wood
Style or Movement: Symbolism
Current Location: Kunsthaus Zürich
⇨

Arnold Böcklin (1827 –1901) was a Swiss symbolist painter. He spent some of his career in Paris and worked at the Louvre and many other places including Rome, Florence, and Zurich.

Symbolism was an artistic movement that suggested ideas through symbols, mythology, and dreams. It began in the late 19th century and was practiced by various painters who rejected the conventions of Naturalism.

This painting portrays St. Anthony as a frustrated preacher reduced to preaching to his only listeners, the fish. The simplistic painting with its stark colors almost reminds one of a modern political cartoon.

Religious significance of the subject matter: St. Anthony converts many when a miracle occurs.

St. Anthony of Padua (1195–1231) was a priest and friar of the Franciscan Order. He was noted for his preaching, miracles, knowledge of scripture, and devotion to the poor. He is the patron saint of finding lost things.

Of the miracle God performed when St. Anthony, being at Rimini, preached to the fishes of the sea

Our Blessed Lord Jesus Christ, wishing to show how holy was his most faithful servant, Saint Anthony, and how devoutly people should listen to his preaching and wholesome teaching, at one time among others rebuked the foolishness of the infidels and the ignorant and the heretics by means of irrational animals – fishes – just as in ancient times in the Old Testament he rebuked the ignorance of Balaam by the mouth of an ass. For once when Saint Anthony was in Rimini, where there was a great number of heretics, wishing to lead them back to the light of the true faith and onto the path of truth, he preached to them for many days and argued about the faith of Christ and about Holy Scripture. But they were stubborn and hard-hearted, and not only did they not accept his holy teaching but, moreover, they refused to listen to him.

So one day, by an inspiration from God, Saint Anthony went to the mouth of the river near the sea. And standing on the bank between the sea and the river, he began to call the fishes in God's name, as for the sermon, saying: "You fishes of the sea and river, listen to the word of God, since the faithless heretics refuse to hear it!"

And as soon as he said that, all of a sudden such a great throng of large and small fishes gathered before him near the bank as had never been seen in that sea or river. And all of them held their heads a bit out of the water, gazing intently at Saint Anthony's face. There you would have seen the big fishes staying close to the little ones, while the smaller ones peacefully swam or stayed under the fins of the larger fishes. You would also have seen the different types of fishes hasten to group themselves together and range themselves before the saint's face like a field painted and adorned with a marvelous variety of colors. You would have seen schools of big fishes occupy the distant places in order to hear the sermon, like an army ranged for battle. You would have seen the middle-sized fishes take their positions in the center and stay in their places without any disturbance, as though they were instructed by God. And you would have seen a great and very dense crowd of small fishes come in a hurry, like pilgrims going to receive an indulgence, and approach closer to the holy father as to their protector. And so first the smaller fishes near the bank, secondly the middle-sized, and thirdly the largest fishes, where the water was deeper, attended this divinely arranged sermon of Saint Anthony – all in very great peace and meekness and order. Then when all the fishes were in their places in perfect order, Saint Anthony solemnly began to preach saying: "My fish brothers, you should give as many thanks as you can to your creator who has granted you such a noble element as your dwelling place, so that you have fresh and salt water, just as you please. Moreover, he has given you many refuges to escape from storms. He has also given you a clear and transparent element and ways to travel and food to live on. Your kind creator also prepares for you the food that you need even in the depths of the ocean. When he created you at the creation of the world, he gave you the command to increase and multiply, and he gave you his blessing. Later during the flood, when all the other animals were perishing, God preserved you alone without loss. He has also given you fins so that with that additional power you can roam wherever you wish. It was granted to you, by order of God, to keep alive Jonas, the prophet of the Lord, and to cast him onto dry land safe and sound on the third day. You offered the tribute money to our Lord Jesus Christ, when as a poor man he had nothing to pay the tax. You were chosen as food for the Eternal King, our blessed Lord Jesus Christ, before his resurrection and in a mysterious way afterwards. Because of all these things you should praise and bless the Lord, who has given you so many more blessings than to other creatures."

At these and similar words and preaching of Saint Anthony, some of the fishes began to open their mouths, and all of them nodded their heads, and by these and other signs of reverence they praised God as much as they could. Then Saint Anthony, seeing how reverent the fishes were toward God the Creator, rejoiced in spirit and cried out in a loud voice: "Blessed be the Eternal God because the fishes of the waters give God more honor than heretical men, and animals lacking reason listen to his word better than faithless men!" And the longer Saint Anthony preached, the more the throng of fishes increased, and not one of them left the place which it had taken. At this miracle the people of the city, including the above-mentioned heretics, came running. And when they saw the marvelous and extraordinary miracle of the fishes listening to Saint Anthony, all of them felt remorse in their hearts, and they sat down at his feet so that he should preach a sermon to them.

Then Saint Anthony preached so wonderfully that he converted and brought back to the faith of Christ all those heretics who were there, and the faithful he sent home with his blessing, strengthened in their faith and filled with joy. Saint Anthony also dismissed the fishes with God's blessing, and they all swam away to various parts of the sea, rejoicing and expressing their joy and applause in amazing games and gambols.

After this, Saint Anthony stayed in Rimini for many days, preaching and reaping much spiritual fruit, both by converting heretics and by stimulating the piety of the clergy.

To the glory of our Lord Jesus Christ who is blessed forever and ever. Amen.
(Attributed to Brother Ugolino, "Of the miracle which God performed when St Anthony, being at Rimini, preached to the fishes of the sea", *The Little Flowers of Saint Francis of Assisi*". Italy: 14th century. https://www.ewtn.com/library/MARY/flowers.htm)

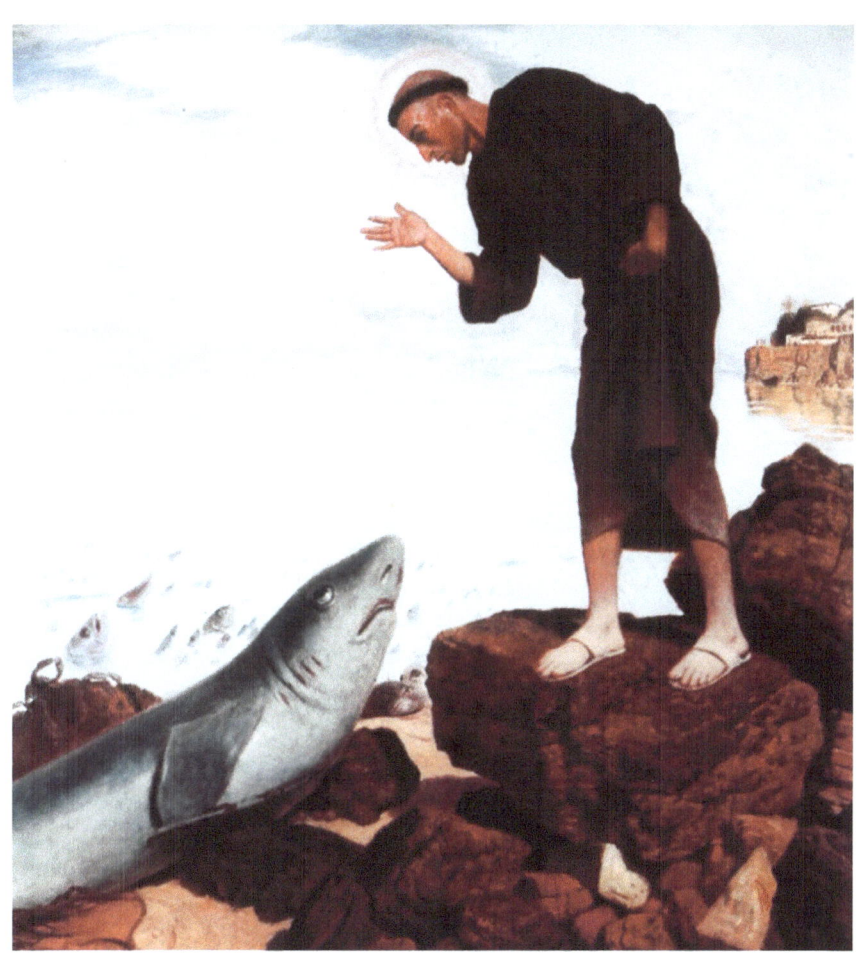

The Queen of the Angels or *The Virgin with Angels*

Artist: William-Adolphe Bouguereau
Date: 1900
Media: oil on canvas
Style or Movement: Traditionalism
Current location: Petit Palais, Paris, France

William-Adolphe Bouguereau (1825-1905) was a French academic painter and traditionalist. He painted realistic figures and chose mythological and occasionally religious themes. Many of his paintings emphasized the female body. He was very popular during his lifetime especially in France and the United States, but in the early 20th century his work fell out of favor. Interest in his art was revived in the latter 20th century.

Traditionalism is the upholding of tradition and resistance to change. Traditionalism in art is in direct opposition to Modernism, which had its beginnings in France in the late 1800's.

This beautiful symmetrical well-known painting shows the Blessed Mother Mary presenting the baby Jesus for all to see and adore. Jesus seems to be blessing and welcoming those who look at the painting with the angels in adoration posing in the form of a halo. The angels each have an individual facial expression and posture. Mary's dark garments portray her as different from her almost glowing child and the brilliant angels.

Religious significance of the subject matter: Mary is Christ's mother and Queen of Heaven.

This painting reminds us of Mary's highly exalted position as the mother of Jesus Christ. She is not only Jesus's physical mother, but she is also filled with God's favor and grace. "And the angel … said unto her: 'Hail, full of grace, the Lord is with thee: blessed art thou among women'" (Luke 1:28, Douay-Rheims Bible).

The Bible also says that all generations will call Mary blessed: "Mary said, 'My soul magnifies the Lord. My spirit has rejoiced in God my Savior, for he has looked at the humble state of his servant. For behold, from now on, all generations will call me blessed. For he who is mighty has done great things for me. Holy is his name'" (Luke 1:46-49).

One of titles given to Mary is Queen of Heaven. This title ties in with this painting, which is entitled "The Queen of the Angels". Mary is thought to be the Queen of Heaven because her son Jesus Christ, is both the son of God and creator along with the Father. St. John Damascene said: "When she became Mother of the Creator, she truly became Queen of every creature."

At the Annunciation, the Archangel Gabriel said to Mary, "He will be great, and will be called the Son of the Most High. The Lord God will give him the throne of his father, David, and he will reign over the house of Jacob forever. There will be no end to his Kingdom" (Luke 1:32-33). Mary's queenship is a share in the kingship of Jesus Christ.

> I saw, and I heard something like a voice of many angels around the throne, the living creatures, and the elders; and the number of them was ten thousands of ten thousands, and thousands of thousands; saying with a loud voice, "Worthy is the Lamb who has been killed to receive the power, wealth, wisdom, strength, honor, glory, and blessing! (Revelation 5:11-12)

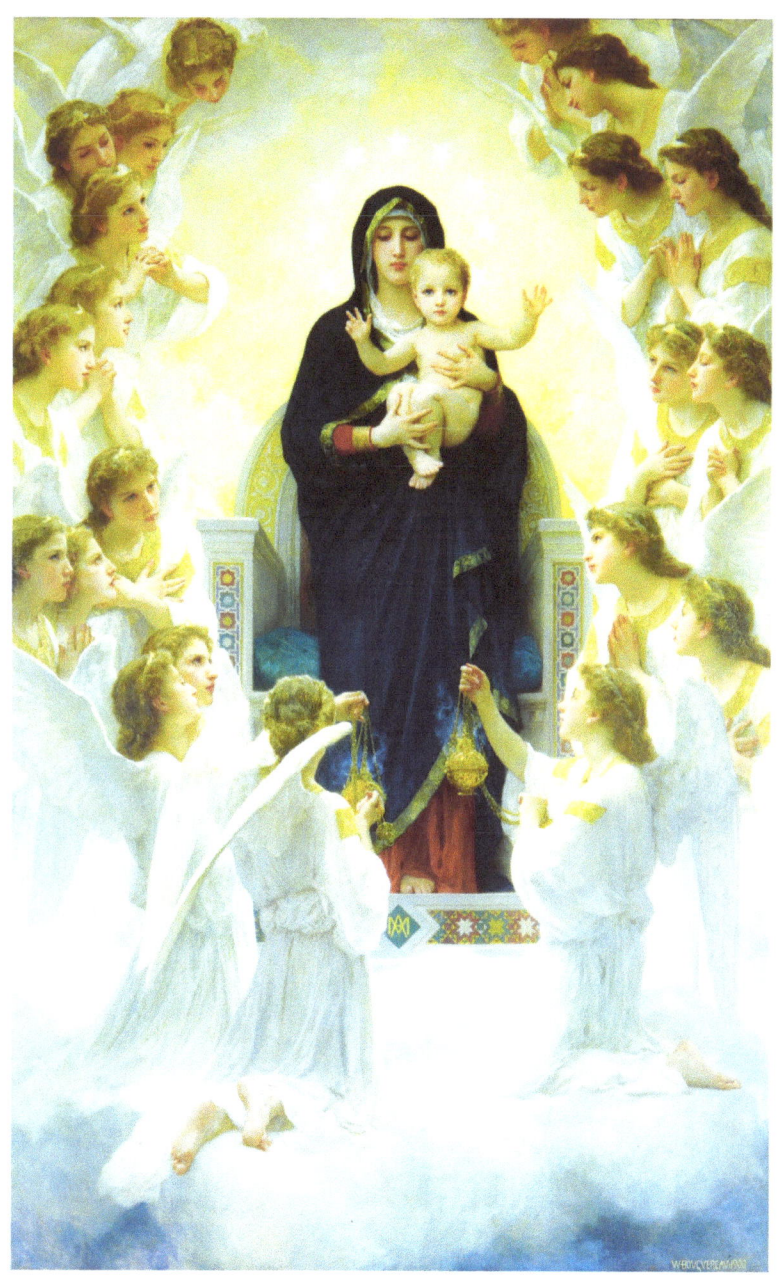

www.ingramcontent.com/pod-product-compliance
Lightning Source LLC
Chambersburg PA
CBHW051217220526
45473CB00003B/1071

9781944158026